Winston Churchill

Winston Churchill

A Biography

Zofia Stone

Alpha Editions

ISBN   :   9789386019509

Design and Setting By
Alpha Editions
email - alphaedis@gmail.com

Contents

Introduction

Sir Winston Leonard Spencer-Churchill, KG, OM, CH, TD, PC, DL, FRS, RA (30 November 1874 – 24 January 1965) was a British statesman who was the Prime Minister of the United Kingdom from 1940 to 1945 and again from 1951 to 1955. Churchill was also an officer in the British Army, a historian, a writer (as Winston S. Churchill), and an artist. He won the Nobel Prize in Literature, and was the first person to be made an honorary citizen of the United States.

Churchill was born into the family of the Dukes of Marlborough, a branch of the Spencer family. His father, Lord Randolph Churchill, was a charismatic politician who served as Chancellor of the Exchequer; his mother, Jennie Jerome, was an American socialite. As a young army officer, he saw action in British India, the Anglo–Sudan War, and the Second Boer War. He gained fame as a war correspondent and wrote books about his campaigns.

At the forefront of politics for fifty years, he held many political and cabinet positions. Before the First World War, he served as President of the Board of Trade, Home Secretary, and First Lord of the Admiralty as part of Asquith's Liberal government. During the war, he continued as First Lord of the Admiralty until the disastrous Gallipoli Campaign caused his departure from government. He then briefly resumed active army service on the Western Front as commander of the 6th Battalion of the Royal Scots Fusiliers. He returned to government under Lloyd George as Minister of Munitions, Secretary of State for War, Secretary of State for Air, then Secretary of State for the Colonies. After two years out of Parliament, he served as Chancellor of the Exchequer in Baldwin's Conservative government of 1924–1929, controversially returning the pound sterling in 1925 to the gold standard at its pre-war parity, a move widely seen as creating deflationary pressure on the UK economy.

Out of office and politically "in the wilderness" during the 1930s because of his opposition to increased home rule for India and his resistance to the 1936 abdication of Edward VIII, Churchill took the lead in warning about Nazi Germany and in campaigning for rearmament. At the outbreak of the Second World War, he was again appointed First Lord of the Admiralty. Following the resignation of Neville Chamberlain on 10 May 1940, Churchill became Prime Minister. His speeches and radio broadcasts helped inspire British resistance, especially during the difficult days of 1940-1 when the British Commonwealth and Empire stood almost alone in its active opposition to Adolf Hitler. He led Britain as Prime Minister until victory over Nazi Germany had been secured.

After the Conservative Party lost the 1945 election, he became Leader of the Opposition to the Labour Government. He publicly warned of an "Iron Curtain" of Soviet influence in Europe and promoted European unity. After winning the 1951 election, Churchill again became Prime Minister. His second term was preoccupied by foreign affairs, including the Malayan Emergency, Mau Mau Uprising, Korean War, and a UK-backed coup d'état in Iran. Domestically his government laid great emphasis on house-building. Churchill suffered a serious stroke in 1953 and retired as Prime Minister in 1955, although he remained a Member of Parliament until 1964. Upon his death aged ninety in 1965, Elizabeth II granted him the honour of a state funeral, which saw one of the largest assemblies of world statesmen in history.[1] Named the Greatest Briton of all time in a 2002 poll, Churchill is widely regarded as being among the most influential people in British history, consistently ranking well in opinion polls of Prime Ministers of the United Kingdom.

EARLY LIFE AND FAMILY

Born into the aristocratic family of the Dukes of Marlborough, a branch of the noble Spencer family, Winston Leonard Spencer-Churchill, like his father, used the surname "Churchill" in public life. His ancestor George Spencer had changed his surname to Spencer-Churchill in 1817 when he became Duke of Marlborough, to highlight his descent from John Churchill, 1st Duke of Marlborough. Churchill's father, Lord Randolph Churchill, the third son of John Spencer-Churchill, 7th Duke of Marlborough, was a politician; and his mother, Lady Randolph Churchill (née Jennie Jerome) was the daughter of American millionaire Leonard Jerome. Churchill was born on 30 November 1874, two months prematurely, in a bedroom in Blenheim Palace, Woodstock, Oxfordshire.

From age two to six, he lived in Dublin, where his grandfather had been appointed Viceroy and employed Churchill's father as his private secretary. Churchill's brother, John Strange Spencer-Churchill, was born during this time in Ireland. It has been claimed that the young Churchill first developed his fascination with military matters from watching the many parades pass by the Vice Regal Lodge (now Áras an Uachtaráin, the official residence of the President of Ireland).

Churchill's earliest exposure to education occurred in Dublin, where a governess tried teaching him reading, writing, and arithmetic (his first reading book was called 'Reading Without Tears'). With limited contact with his parents, Churchill became very close to his nanny, 'Mrs' Elizabeth Ann Everest, whom he called 'Old Woom'. She served as his confidante, nurse, and mother substitute. The two spent many happy hours playing in Phoenix Park.

Independent and rebellious by nature, Churchill generally

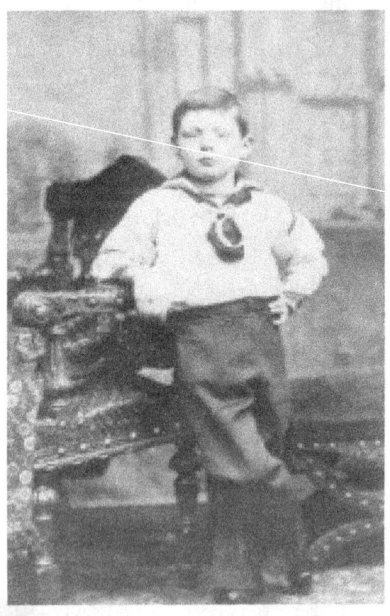

Churchill, aged seven, in 1881

had a poor academic record in school, for which he was punished. He was educated at three independent schools: St. George's School, Ascot, Berkshire; Brunswick School in Hove, near Brighton (the school has since been renamed Stoke Brunswick School and relocated to Ashurst Wood in West Sussex); and at Harrow School from 17 April 1888. Within weeks of his arrival at Harrow, Churchill had joined the Harrow Rifle Corps.

When young Winston started attending Harrow School, he was listed under the S's as Spencer Churchill. At that time Winston was a stocky boy with red hair who talked with a stutter and a lisp. Winston did so well in mathematics in his Harrow entrance exam that he was put in the top division for that subject. In his first year at Harrow he was recognized as being the best in his division for history. Winston entered the school, however, as the boy with the lowest grades in the lowest class, and he remained in that position. Winston never even made it into the upper school because he would not study the classics. Though he did poorly in his schoolwork, he grew to love the English language. He hated Harrow. His mother rarely visited him, and he wrote letters begging her either to come to the school or to allow him to come home. His relationship with his father was distant; he once remarked that they barely spoke to one another. His father died on 24 January 1895, aged 45, leaving Churchill with the conviction that he too would die young and so should be quick about making his mark on the world.

At age 18, while visiting his aunt Lady Wimborne in

Bournemouth, Winston nearly died when he fell from a bridge over a seaside chine (either Branksome Dene or Alum Chine) at a height of 29 feet. As a result of injuries sustained in the fall, he was unconscious for three days and bedridden for three months. Winston Churchill was a member of the freemasons and a member of the Loyal Waterloo Lodge of the National Independent Order of Odd Fellows.

Churchill had a lateral lisp that continued throughout his career, reported consistently by journalists of the time and later. Authors writing in the 1920s and 1930s, before sound recording became common, also mentioned Churchill having a stutter, describing it in terms such as "severe" or "agonising". The Churchill Centre and Museum says the majority of records show his impediment was a lateral lisp, while Churchill's stutter is a myth. His dentures were specially designed to aid his speech (Demosthenes' pebbles). After many years of public speeches carefully prepared not only to inspire, but also to avoid hesitations, he could finally state, "My impediment is no hindrance".

Marriage

Churchill met his future wife, Clementine Hozier, in 1904 at a ball in Crewe House, home of the Earl of Crewe and Crewe's wife Margaret Primrose (daughter of Archibald Primrose, 5th Earl of Rosebery, and Hannah Rothschild). In 1908, they met again at a dinner party hosted by Susan Jeune, Baroness St Helier. Churchill found himself seated beside Clementine, and they soon began a lifelong romance. He proposed to Clementine during a house party at Blenheim Palace on 10 August 1908, in a small Temple of Diana. On 12 September 1908, he and Clementine were married in St. Margaret's, Westminster. The church was packed; the Bishop of St Asaph conducted the service. The couple spent their honeymoon at Highgrove House in Eastcote. In March 1909, the couple moved to a house at 33 Eccleston Square.

Their first child, Diana, was born in London on 11 July 1909. After the pregnancy, Clementine moved to Sussex to recover, while Diana stayed in London with her nanny. On 28 May 1911, their second child, Randolph, was born at 33 Eccleston Square.

Their third child, Sarah, was born on 7 October 1914 at Admiralty House. The birth was marked with anxiety for Clementine, as Churchill had been sent to Antwerp by the Cabinet to "stiffen the resistance of the beleaguered city" after news that the Belgians intended to surrender the town. Clementine gave birth to her fourth child, Marigold Frances Churchill, on 15 November 1918, four days after the official end of the First World War. In the early days of August 1921, the Churchills' children were entrusted to a French nursery governess in Kent named Mlle. Rose. Clementine, meanwhile, travelled to Eaton Hall to play tennis with Hugh Grosvenor, 2nd Duke of Westminster, and his family. While still under the care of Mlle. Rose, Marigold had a cold, but was reported to have recovered from the illness. As the illness progressed with hardly any notice, it turned into septicaemia. Following advice from a landlady, Rose sent for Clementine. However the illness proved fatal on 23 August 1921, and Marigold was buried in the Kensal Green Cemetery three days later. On 15 September 1922, the Churchills' last child, Mary, was born. Later that month, the Churchills bought Chartwell, which would be their home until Winston's death.

MILITARY SERVICE

After Churchill left Harrow in 1893, he applied to attend the Royal Military College, Sandhurst. He tried three times before passing the entrance exam; he applied to be trained for the cavalry rather than the infantry because the required grade was lower and he was not required to learn mathematics, which he disliked. He graduated eighth out of a class of 150 in December 1894, and although he could now have transferred to an infantry regiment as his father had wished, chose to remain with the cavalry and was commissioned as a cornet (second lieutenant) in the 4th Queen's Own Hussars on 20 February 1895. In 1941, he received the honour of being appointed Regimental Colonel of the 4th Hussars, an honour which was increased after the Second World War when he was appointed as Colonel-in-Chief; this privilege is usually reserved for members of the royal family.

Churchill's pay as a second lieutenant in the 4th Hussars was £300 annually. However, he believed that he needed at least a further £500 to support a style of life equal to that of other officers of the regiment. His mother provided an allowance of £400 per year, but this was repeatedly overspent. According to biographer Roy Jenkins, this is one reason why he took an interest in war correspondence. He did not intend to follow a conventional career of promotion through army ranks, but rather to seek out all possible chances of military action, using his mother's and family influence in high society to arrange postings to active campaigns. His writings brought him to the attention of the public, and earned him significant additional income. He acted as a war correspondent for several London newspapers and wrote his own books about the campaigns.

Churchill in military uniform, 1895

Cuba

In 1895, during the Cuban War of Independence, Churchill, and fellow officer Reginald Barnes, travelled to Cuba to observe the Spanish fight the Cuban guerrillas; he had obtained a commission to write about the conflict from the Daily Graphic. He came under fire on his twenty-first birthday, the first of about 50 times during his life, and the Spanish awarded him his first medal.:17 Churchill had fond memories of Cuba as a "... large, rich, beautiful island ...". While there, he soon acquired a taste for Havana cigars, which he would smoke for the rest of his life. While in New York, he stayed at the home of Bourke Cockran, an admirer of his mother. Bourke was an established American politician, and a member of the House of Representatives. He greatly influenced Churchill, both in his approach to oratory and politics, and encouraging a love of America.

He soon received word that his nanny, Mrs Everest, was dying; he then returned to England and stayed with her for a week until she died. He wrote in his journal, "She was my favourite friend." In My Early Life he wrote: "She had been my dearest and most intimate friend during the whole of the twenty years I had lived."

India

In early October 1896, he was transferred to Bombay, British India. He was considered one of the best polo players in his regiment and led his team to many prestigious tournament victories. Churchill came to Bangalore in 1896 as a young army officer, before leaving three years later for the North West Frontier to fight in the Second Anglo-Afghan War. In his book, 'My Early Life', he describes Bangalore as a city with excellent weather, and his allotted house as 'a magnificent pink and white stucco palace in the middle of a large and beautiful garden' with servants, dhobi (to wash clothes), gardener, watchman and a water-carrier. It was in Bangalore he met Pamela Plowden, daughter of a civil servant; she became his first love.

In 1897, Churchill attempted to travel to both report on and, if necessary, fight in the Greco-Turkish War, but this conflict effectively ended before he could arrive. Later, while preparing for a leave in England, he heard that three brigades of the British Army were going to fight against a Pashtun tribe in the North West Frontier of India and he asked his superior officer if he could join the fight. He fought under the command of General Jeffery, the commander of the second brigade operating in Malakand, in the Frontier region of British India. Jeffery sent him with fifteen scouts to explore the Mamund Valley; while on reconnaissance, they encountered an enemy tribe, dismounted from their horses and opened fire. After an hour of shooting, their reinforcements, the 35th Sikhs arrived, the firing gradually ceased and the brigade and the Sikhs marched on. Hundreds of tribesmen then ambushed them and opened fire, forcing them to retreat. As they were retreating, four men were carrying an injured officer, but the fierceness of the fight forced them to leave him behind. The man who was left behind was slashed to death before Churchill's eyes; afterwards he wrote of the killer, "I forgot everything else at this moment except a desire to kill this man." However, the Sikhs' numbers were being depleted, so the next commanding officer told Churchill to get the rest of the men to safety.

Before he left, he asked for a note so that he would not be charged with desertion. He received the note, quickly signed, headed up the hill and alerted the other brigade, whereupon they then engaged the army. The fighting in the region dragged on for another two weeks before the dead could be recovered. He wrote in his journal: "Whether it was worth it I cannot tell." An account of the Siege of Malakand was published in December 1900 as The Story of the Malakand Field Force. He received £600 for his account. During the campaign, he also wrote articles for the newspapers The Pioneer and The Daily Telegraph. His account of the battle was one of his first published stories, for which he received £5 per column from The Daily Telegraph.

Sudan

Churchill was transferred to Egypt in 1898. He visited Luxor before joining an attachment of the 21st Lancers serving in the Sudan under the command of General Herbert Kitchener. During this time he encountered two military officers with whom he would work during the First World War: Douglas Haig, then a captain, and David Beatty, then a gunboat lieutenant. While in the Sudan, he participated in what has been described as the last meaningful British cavalry charge, at the Battle of Omdurman in September 1898. He also worked as a war correspondent for the Morning Post. By October 1898, he had returned to Britain and begun his two-volume work, The River War, an account of the conquest of the Sudan which was published the following year. Churchill resigned from the British Army effective from 5 May 1899.

Oldham

He soon had his first opportunity to begin a Parliamentary career, when he was invited by Robert Ascroft to be the second Conservative Party candidate in Ascroft's Oldham constituency. Ascroft's sudden death caused a double by-election and Churchill was one of the candidates. In the midst of a national trend against the Conservatives, both seats were lost; however, Churchill impressed by his vigorous campaigning.

South Africa

Having failed at Oldham, Churchill looked about for some other opportunity to advance his career. On 12 October 1899, the Second Boer War between Britain and the Boer Republics broke out and he obtained a commission to act as war correspondent for The Morning Post with a salary of £250 per month. He rushed to sail on the same ship as the newly appointed British commander, Sir Redvers Buller. After some weeks in exposed areas, he accompanied a scouting expedition in an armoured train, leading to his capture and imprisonment in a POW camp in Pretoria (converted school building for

Pretoria High School for Girls). His actions during the ambush of the train led to speculation that he would be awarded the Victoria Cross, Britain's highest award to members of the armed forces for gallantry in the face of the enemy, but this was not possible, as he was a civilian. He escaped from the prison camp and, with the assistance of an English mine manager, travelled almost 300 miles (480 km) to safety in Portuguese East Africa. His escape made him a minor national hero for a time in Britain though, instead of returning home, he rejoined General Buller's army on its march to relieve the British at the Siege of Ladysmith and take Pretoria. This time, although continuing as a war correspondent, he gained a commission in the South African Light Horse. He was among the first British troops into Ladysmith and Pretoria. He and his cousin, the Duke of Marlborough, were able to get ahead of the rest of the troops in Pretoria, where they demanded and received the surrender of 52 Boer prison camp guards.

In 1900, Churchill returned to England on the RMS Dunottar Castle, the same ship on which he had set sail for South Africa eight months earlier. The same year he published London to Ladysmith and a second volume of Boer war experiences, Ian Hamilton's March.

Territorial Service and advancement

In 1900, he retired from the regular army, and in 1902 joined the Imperial Yeomanry, where he was commissioned as a Captain in the Queen's Own Oxfordshire Hussars on 4 January 1902. In that same year, he was initiated into Freemasonry at

Studholme Lodge #1591, London, and raised to the Third Degree on 25 March 1902. In April 1905, he was promoted to Major and appointed to command of the Henley Squadron of the Queen's Own Oxfordshire Hussars. In September 1916, he transferred to the territorial reserves of officers, where he remained until retiring in 1924, at the age of fifty.

Western Front

After his resignation from the government in 1915, Churchill rejoined the British Army, attempting to obtain an appointment as brigade commander, but settling for command of a battalion. After spending some time as a Major with the 2nd Battalion, Grenadier Guards, he was appointed Lieutenant-Colonel, commanding the 6th Battalion, Royal Scots Fusiliers (part of the 9th (Scottish) Division), on 1 January 1916. Correspondence with his wife shows that his intent in taking up active service was to rehabilitate his reputation, but this was balanced by the serious risk of being killed. During his period of command, his battalion was stationed at Ploegsteert but did not take part in any set battle. Although he disapproved strongly of the mass slaughter involved in many Western Front actions, he exposed himself to danger by making excursions to the front line or into No Man's Land.

POLITICAL CAREER AND PATH TO THE SECOND WORLD WAR

Churchill entered Parliament as member for Oldham in 1900 as a Conservative. He changed parties in 1904 after increasing disagreement with the mainstream Conservative policy of protectionist tariffs preferentially favouring trade with the British Empire, joining the Liberals and winning the seat of Manchester North West. His political ascent was rapid, becoming successively Under-Secretary of State for the Colonies, President of the Board of Trade, Home Secretary, and First Lord of the Admiralty before he was 40 years old. His career suffered a severe check in 1915, after his support for the failed Dardanelles Campaign during World War I, and the subsequent formation of the first Coalition. Temporarily leaving politics, he served on the Western Front before rejoining the Government after David Lloyd George had replaced H. H. Asquith as prime minister. He served as Minister of Munitions, Secretary of State for War, Secretary of State for Air, and Secretary of State for the Colonies before the downfall of the Coalition in 1922 when he also lost his seat in Parliament.

After contesting two seats unsuccessfully as an independent, he was elected to Epping in 1924 with the backing of local Conservatives, officially rejoining the Conservative Party the following year. He immediately became Chancellor of the Exchequer, retaining the post until the fall of the Conservative government in 1929, and presided over the return of the United Kingdom to the Gold Standard exchange rate system. In opposition after 1929, Churchill became isolated, opposing Indian independence, advocating the unpopular policy of rearmament in the face of a resurgent Germany, and supporting King Edward VIII in the abdication crisis. By 1939, he had been out of Cabinet for ten years, and his career seemed all but over.

Early years in Parliament

His first political appearance was at a meeting of the Conservative Primrose League, in Bath in 1897, while at home on leave from the army in India. Having discovered that the Conservative Party needed speakers, as he later commented: "I surveyed the prospect with the eye of an urchin looking through a pastrycook's window."

The speech concerned the benefits to the working man of "Tory Democracy" and was reported in the Morning Post.

Member for Oldham

His first attempt to enter Parliament was unsuccessful when

in July 1899 he was defeated in a by-election for the seat of Oldham in Lancashire. The constituency returned two members of parliament, both Conservatives at the previous election. One of them was ill and sought to retire, and Churchill was chosen as the new candidate. However, before the election the second member died so that two new candidates stood against two respected Liberal candidates, at a time when the popularity of the Conservative government was in decline.

Churchill looked about for a way to improve his public standing after the defeat. He arranged to travel as a war correspondent to South Africa, fortified by a letter of recommendation to the high commissioner, Alfred Milner, from the Colonial Secretary, Joseph Chamberlain, who had been a friend of his father, and by a promise of a military attachment. His reputation was considerably improved by his war reports published in national newspapers, and by his own military exploits, particularly his capture by and escape from the Boers.

He stood again for Oldham in the 1900 general election, known as "the Khaki election" because the Conservative government greatly benefited from its success in the Boer war.:23–24 This time he came second, pushing one of the Liberal candidates into third place, and was elected. In both of these elections, his campaign expenses were paid for by his cousin the 9th Duke of Marlborough.

Churchill chose not to attend the opening of Parliament in December 1900 and instead embarked on a speaking tour throughout Britain and the United States. With the success of his tour and through his prolific writing in various journals and books, he earned £10,000 for himself in 1899 and 1900 (equivalent to around £500,000 in 2001).:69–70 Members of Parliament were unpaid and Churchill had inherited almost no money; the income he did inherit from his father's estate, he assigned to his mother in 1903.:26 He took his seat in parliament in February 1901.

Crossing the floor

In Parliament, Churchill became associated with a group of Tory dissidents led by Lord Hugh Cecil called the Hughligans, a play on words with "hooligans". His first major speech in Parliament was an attack on the proposal of Secretary of State for War St John Broderick to expand the army to six corps, three of which would be free to form an expeditionary force overseas. Churchill had prepared his speech for over six weeks and spoke for an hour without notes. The speech showed his rhetorical powers and was compared by commentators at the time to that of his father's first success – also an attack on a cabinet minister of his own party. Churchill maintained the campaign in and out of Parliament for some time. In 1902, Churchill revealed some of his views in an interview at the University of Michigan only published six decades later. In the interview, he spoke candidly about his desire for "the ultimate partition of China", as "the Aryan stock is bound to triumph." He also expressed lack of concern for Russian expansion towards China and India, as "Russia has a justifiable ambition to possess a warm water port. It is really embarrassing to think that 100,000,000 people are without one" - an unusual view during the era of the Great Game.

By 1903, he was drawing away from Lord Hugh's views, although they remained friends – Lord Hugh was Churchill's best man in 1908. He also opposed the Liberal Unionist leader Joseph Chamberlain, whose party was in coalition with the Conservatives. Chamberlain proposed extensive tariffs intended to protect Britain's economic dominance. Churchill then and later supported free trade. In this he was supported by Lord Hugh and other Conservatives, including the then Chancellor of the Exchequer C. T. Ritchie. Chamberlain's Tariff Reform movement gained strength splitting the Conservative-Unionist alliance. Churchill's attacks on the Conservatives continued on a number of topics, his dissatisfaction had many causes.:ch 2 His dissatisfaction grew, he made personal attacks on some of the leaders, including Chamberlain, and was reciprocated; Conservative backbenchers staged a walkout once while he was speaking.:86 and many were personally hostile to him.:28 His own constituency effectively deselected him, the Conservative Association passing a resolution that he "had forfeited their confidence in him." Oldham was an important cotton-spinning centre whose electorate favoured the Unionist policy of Protectionism, which advocated duties on cheap foreign textiles. He continued to sit for Oldham until the next general election.

In 1904, Churchill's dissatisfaction had grown so strong that, on returning from the Whitsun recess, he crossed the floor of the House of Commons to sit as a member of the Liberal Party. His cousin Ivor Guest followed him. Suggested reasons for Churchill's changing sides have included the prospect of a ministerial post and salary,:27 a desire to eliminate poverty, and concerns for the working class, but the immediately preceding events were the rift with the Conservative Party over trade tariffs. He may simply have been more sympathetic to the Liberals, despite being personally conservative and traditionalist; in 1962 he reportedly told another MP "I'm a Liberal. Always have been.":24 As a Liberal, he continued to campaign for free trade.

That resemblance went far; Churchill dressed like his father, and the Hughiglans have been seen as the recreation of Lord Randolph's Fourth Party. From 1903 until 1905, Churchill was also engaged in writing Lord Randolph Churchill, a two-volume biography of his father which was published in 1906 and received much critical acclaim.:102–103 However, filial devotion caused him to soften some of his father's less attractive aspects.:101 Theodore Roosevelt, who had known Lord Randolph, reviewed the book as "a clever, tactful, and rather cheap and vulgar life of that clever, tactful, and rather cheap and vulgar egotist".:47 Historians suggest Churchill used the book in part to vindicate his own career and in particular to justify crossing the floor.:41:34–35 Churchill himself later wrote that studying his father's life was a major cause of his disenchantment with the Conservatives.

Growing prominence

When the Liberals took office, with Henry Campbell-Bannerman as Prime Minister, in December 1905, Churchill became Under-Secretary of State for the Colonies. Serving under the Secretary of State for the Colonies, Victor Bruce, 9th Earl of Elgin, Churchill dealt with the adoption of constitutions for the defeated Boer republics of the Transvaal and Orange River Colony and with the issue of 'Chinese slavery' in South African mines. His first speech after taking office, in which he tried to defend Lord Milner while opposing his policies was a failure. Churchill had prepared it in advance, he had rehearsed it before his private secretary. While the speech reads well, it was not suited to the mood of the House, and the Conservatives proclaimed that Churchill was finished.:19:38–39 It was a failure of his technique of writing his speeches in advance. But he learned from his mistakes. In the 1906 general election, he won the seat of Manchester North West (carefully selected for him by the party). His electoral expenses were paid for by his uncle Lord Tweedmouth, a senior Liberal.

Churchill had become one of the most prominent members of the Government outside the Cabinet. Indeed, Campbell-Bannerman had proposed his promotion to the Cabinet while Churchill was still Undersecretary, but the King vetoed his appointment.:181 When Campbell-Bannerman was succeeded by Herbert Henry Asquith in 1908, he was promoted to the Cabinet as President of the Board of Trade. Under the law at the time, a newly appointed Cabinet Minister was obliged to seek re-election at a by-election. Churchill lost his Manchester seat to the Conservative William Joynson-Hicks. Almost one third of the seat were Jewish and many others were Roman Catholic. The Liberals' adoption of the Alien Act and Churchill's refusal to commit to Home Rule together with

Churchill's concentration on national rather than local issues are given as the reason for his defeat. He was soon elected in another by-election at Dundee constituency.

As President of the Board of Trade he supported David Lloyd George, the newly appointed Chancellor of the Exchequer, in opposing the 1908-9 naval estimates. The First Lord of the Admiralty, Reginald McKenna proposed six dreadnoughts. Lloyd George, with Churchill's support wanted only four. But a public campaign led by the Conservatives with covert support from First Sea Lord Jackie Fisher, who was a Liberal appointment, forced the government to order eight. Churchill gave speeches on this issue, referring to his father's campaign for economy, and circulated open letters to his constituents (again following his father's practise).:41–42

Also as President of the Board of Trade, Churchill took an active role in bringing about the radical social reforms which have become known as the Liberal reforms. The first of these, passed while Churchill was still Colonial Undersecretary, the Trade Disputes Act 1906 overturned the Taff Vale Case by providing that unions were not liable for damages caused by strike action. His direct achievements at the Board of Trade were considerable particularly in employment law. He was responsible for the Mines Act 1908, which provided for an 8-hour day in all mines; the Trades Boards Act 1909, which established the first minimum wage system in Britain, mandating rates for both time- and piece-work for 200,000 workers in several industries (Churchill was able to get Conservative support for this and the Bill "passed without a division.") and the Labour Exchanges Act 1909, setting up offices to help unemployed people find work.:150–151 As Home Secretary he continued these reforms with the National Insurance Act 1911, providing sickness and unemployment benefits. As a Cabinet Minister he had three outstanding qualities: he worked hard, he carried his proposals through Cabinet and Parliament, and he carried his department with him. These qualities, the historian, parliamentary clerk, and politician Robert Rhodes James notes, are not as common as they should be.:43 Churchill himself put his advancement to his submissions to Cabinet, not to his speeches.

Churchill's most important indirect role in these reforms was his assistance in passing the People's Budget and the Parliament Act of 1911.:157–166 The Budget included the introduction of new taxes on the wealthy to fund new social welfare programmes. Churchill biographer William Manchester called the People's Budget "a revolutionary concept" because it was the first budget in British history with the expressed intent of redistributing wealth to the British public. When the Budget was discussed in 1909 he did feel some ambiguity over it.:159 But despite his doubts about its effectiveness, he launched himself into the fight for the budget and accepted the presidency of the Budget League, an organisation set up in response to the opposition's "Budget Protest League".:161

After the budget was sent to the Commons in 1909 and passed, it went to the House of Lords, where it was subsequently vetoed. The Liberals than fought and won two general elections in January and December 1910 to gain a mandate for their reforms. In these campaigns which resulted in the curbing of the Lords' veto by the Parliament Act, Churchill was again to the fore, adding humour in his speeches.

In 1909 Churchill published a collection of speeches with a foreword under the title Liberalism and the Social Problem. In it he argued for maintaining much of the social order and for gradualism in reform. He wanted to make the existing society work better and more humanely so as to preserve it better. Churchill, it was said, wanted a society where the upper class remained in control, distributing benefits to a grateful and industrious working class.:44–46 He was then compared with Lloyd George who was seen as Churchill's mentor and from whom Churchill learned much, but who, unlike Churchill, wanted to change some of the fundamental structures of society. Churchill was one of very few Liberals who pressed for the expansion of the House of Lords whether or not the Parliament Act was passed.

Home Secretary

In 1910, Churchill was promoted to Home Secretary. His term was marked by three main controversies: a violent Rhondda coalminers' strike and industrial relations issues generally, his responses to the Siege of Sidney Street and the suffragettes agitation.

In 1910, coalminers in the Rhondda Valley began what has come to be known as the Tonypandy Riots. Initially, the chief constable of Glamorgan requested that troops be sent in to help police quell the rioting. Churchill, when he learned that they had been sent, allowed them to go as far as Swindon and Cardiff and authorised the commanding general to advance further if he should judge it necessary. Churchill, who had already forbidden the use of forces in another industrial dispute at Newport, did not favour deployment of troops, fearing a repeat of the 1887 Bloody Sunday in Trafalgar Square. In particular, Churchill forbade the use of troops as strike breakers.:48 On 9 November, the Times leader criticised this decision, saying that responsibility for the "renewed rioting late last night...will lie with the Home Secretary (Churchill)" for countermanding the chief constable's request for troops. In spite of this, the rumour persisted that Churchill had ordered troops to attack, and Churchill's reputation in Wales and in Labour circles never recovered.

In early January 1911, Churchill arrived at the "Siege of Sidney Street" in London. He gave his own account of the incident in his book Thoughts and Adventures. There is some uncertainty as to whether Churchill attempted to give operational commands. Biographer Roy Jenkins comments that the reason he went was because "he could not resist going to see the fun himself" and that he did not issue commands.:194 A famous photograph from the time shows Churchill at the scene, peering around a corner to view the gun battle between cornered anarchists and Scots Guards. His role and presence attracted much criticism. The building under siege caught fire, and Churchill supported the decision to deny the fire brigade access, forcing the criminals to choose surrender or death. After an inquest, Arthur Balfour remarked, " Churchill] and a photographer were both risking valuable lives. I understand what the photographer was doing but what was the Right Honourable gentleman doing?":195 The significance was that the whole highly publicised affair increased Churchill's already incipient reputation for being a frenetic and far-from-calm Home Secretary. While still at the Board of Trade in 1909, Churchill was accosted with a whip by suffragette Theresa Garnett.:186:237 Churchill's proposed solution was a referendum on the issue but this found no favour with Herbert Henry Asquith and women's suffrage remained unresolved until after World War I.:186

First Lord of the Admiralty

In 1911, Churchill was transferred to the office of the First Lord of the Admiralty, a post he held into World War I. This was the year of the Agadir Crisis, with which Churchill opens The World Crisis, his account of World War One. His first major act was to replace all but one of the Sea Lords, the senior naval officers who administered the Admiralty. With the aid of the new First Sea Lord Sir Francis Bridgeman he created a war staff,:ch IV gave impetus to reform efforts, including development of naval aviation (he undertook flying lessons himself), the use of the 15" gun as the main armament of battleships, the development of the fast battleship (which found shape in the Queen Elizabeth class) and of the 6" gunned light cruiser (which found shape in the Arethusa class) concepts,:ch 4, 6 and the switch from coal to oil in the Royal Navy, a massive engineering task, which depended on securing oil supplies in Mesopotamia. In 1912, in response to the German Naval Law of that year, Churchill brought forward Naval Estimates based on a principle of building two British battleships to every one German, which became known as 'two keels to one."

Churchill was influenced in these reforms by the (then-retired) Admiral of the Fleet Lord Fisher, who had been for many years a driving force for innovation in the Royal Navy. The two men had become very close at Biarritz in April 1907. In 1909, Fisher had been First Sea Lord and on the opposite side to Churchill in the debates over the Naval Estimates. However this was a temporary tension, and the friendship persisted. Fisher remained in close touch with naval affairs after his retirement from the Admiralty in January 1910, and Churchill consulted him almost instantly upon taking up the office of First Lord.:431–32 Many of the ideas Churchill took up, like oil propulsion and ever-bigger battleships with ever-bigger guns, were causes Fisher backed with his peculiar drive; however other Fisher proposals, like an expansion of the submarine fleet or the introduction of diesel engines to capital ships, got nowhere.:435–37

In 1912 the Liberal Government, since the elections in 1910 dependent upon Irish National support, introduced what became the Home Rule Act 1914. The Unionists (the Conservatives and Liberal Unionists had united in 1911) bitterly opposed this, demanding that Ulster be excluded from the Home Rule Parliament. Privately Churchill sought a compromise.:57 Publicly (and particularly after Sir Edward

Carson's Ulster Covenant by which over half a million men pledged to oppose Home Rule by 'all means which shall be found necessary' and the formation of the Ulster Volunteers), he campaigned for the Bill by speeches in Ulster and England and open letters.:58 This caused great anger among the Unionists because Lord Randolph had been the champion of Ulster against Parnell's original Home Rule campaign.

As the crisis deepened, with the Ulster Volunteers drilling openly, Churchill arranged for a Royal Naval battleship squadron to cruise off Belfast:148 without first raising the issue in Cabinet. Asquith cancelled the move two days later.:63 The cancellation is not mentioned in The Gathering Storm. It appeared to the Unionist leaders that Churchill and his friend War Secretary John Seely were seeking to provoke the Unionists into some outward act that would allow Ulster to be placed under some form of military rule. The attempts to move troops led to the Curragh Incident, Seely's resignation, a backdown by the Government, and negotiations brokered by King George V. This incident revealed for the first time that Churchill was not prepared to negotiate under pressure, that while he would compromise behind the scenes and be magnanimous in victory, when confronted by a foe he stood his ground.

World War I

On 31 July 1914, Churchill ordered the seizure of the two Turkish battleships then under construction in Britain. Although this decision was probably a wise one,:74 the way the order was carried out was not. The ships were boarded without negotiations with Turkey or compensation, and the British placed guards on one of the battleships to prevent Turkish sailors from boarding. The order probably helped propel Turkey into alliance with Germany. (Two German warships arriving in Turkey were portrayed as replaacements.) Churchill later defended himself referring to the negotiations that the Germans were starting with the Young Turks.:169 But Britain was also negotiating with Turkey at the same time and on 18 August Turkey declared neutrality.

In September 1914, Joffre suggested that the British create a 'demonstration' at Dunkirk to distract German forces from Joffre's plans which culminated in the Battle of the Marne. Churchill at Kitchener's suggestion took charge of a mixed force of Yeomanry and Marines. He arranged for 50 London buses to be used for extra mobility and the troops were used in general operations for a few weeks until the "Circus" was wound up. On 5 October 1914, Churchill went to Antwerp, which the Belgian government proposed to evacuate and surrender to the Germans. The Royal Marine Brigade was there, and at Churchill's urgings the 1st and 2nd Naval Brigades were also committed. Churchill proposed to resign from the Admiralty and take executive command of the newly formed Royal Naval Division, which incorporated the Marine and Naval Brigades. His offer, supported by Kitchener, who wanted to commit an Anglo-French expeditionary force to secure Antwerp,:320 was rejected by the Cabinet. Antwerp fell on 10 October 1914 with the loss of 2,500 men.

At the time Churchill was attacked for squandering

resources. His defence was that the British force had prolonged resistance in Antwerp by five days and occupied five German divisions.:323 It is more likely that his actions prolonged the resistance by a week (Belgium had proposed surrendering Antwerp on 3 October), and that this delay saved Calais and Dunkirk.:80 The more damaging attack, made inside and outside the Cabinet, was that Churchill was seeking publicity instead of running his department.

He was also unpopular within the Navy itself for the replacement of Sir George Callaghan by Sir John Jellicoe as commander of the Grand Fleet and for bowing to public pressure and dismissing Prince Louis of Battenberg as First Sea Lord, although he was one of the last members of the government to concede that Battenberg had to be replaced.

Early development of the tank

Churchill sponsored the development of the tank, which was financed from naval research funds. After witnessing a demonstration in which an armoured tractor successfully cut through a barbed wire entanglement, Churchill and Lloyd George decided that tanks could prove useful. Churchill then headed the Landships Committee which was responsible for creating the first tank corps and, although a decade later development of the battle tank would be seen as a tactical victory, at the time it was seen as misappropriation of funds. The tank was deployed too early and in too small numbers, much to Churchill's annoyance. He wanted a fleet of tanks used to surprise the Germans under cover of smoke, and to

open a large section of the trenches by crushing barbed wire
and creating a breakthrough sector

Dardanelles Campaign

In early 1915, Churchill campaigned for an amphibious
assault on the Belgian coast in 1914, which was opposed by
Lord Kitchener at the War Office and Sir John French
commanding the British Expeditionary Force. Churchill then
became one of the political and military engineers of the
disastrous Gallipoli Campaign.

In 1911, Churchill had written that "it is no longer possible
to force the Dardanelles". Nonetheless, Churchill and others
in the Admiralty, including Admiral Oliver, the Chief of the
Naval Staff, were impressed by the German bombardment of
Belgian fortresses in the Battle of Liège at the start of the war.
As early as August 1914, he had ordered an appreciation of "a
plan for the seizure of the Gallipoli peninsula, by a Greek
army of adequate strength, with a view to admitting a British
fleet to the Sea of Marmara." This was some three months
before Turkey was at war and more than two years before
Greece entered the war. Although later in August Greece did
offer to attack Turkey, the offer was not accepted by Britain
due to complaints from its ally Russia, and was withdrawn
before Turkey entered the war in October.

Churchill pressed the issue at successive meetings of the
War Council in 1914. After an exchange of telegrams with

Admiral Sackville Carden, the Commander in the Aegean, he tabled his plan for forcing the Straits by naval bombardment at a further meeting of the Council in January 1915. He had not sought the view of the Naval Staff, and those senior naval officers with whom he had discussed the plan were dubious or opposed to the scheme.:85 The concept was flawed. The first attacks by the Navy in February 1915 were successful but were not pressed home (partly because of bad weather) and no troops were available to secure the gains made. Instead marines blew up the outer forts, which were reoccupied and rebuilt when the marines left.:163 The War Council had discussed using the 29th Division (then in Britain) and the Australian and New Zealand Army Corps (then in Egypt) but no decision had been made when the naval attacks began.:89 At the time, Churchill claimed the navy could do the job alone and the troops would be needed - if at all – as an occupying force once the Straits were forced. Carden's attack was slowed because the inner forts were concealed from the ships and few aircraft were available for spotting purposes (the seaplane tender HMS Ark Royal which supported the fleet carried just five seaplanes of an older design lacking sufficient range). Carden asked to discontinue the attack until there were more available.

Churchill refused, requiring the attack to continue, and Carden planned to continue but then collapsed from a rupturing ulcer. His second in command, Admiral John de Robeck took over and pressed a further attack on 18 March, but this failed when the trawler minesweepers crewed by Royal Naval Volunteer Reserves (i.e. civilian seamen) came under attack and then the battleships ran into a mine field (three were sunk).

De Robeck did not repeat the attacks, later giving his reason as concerns over what would happen if his ships succeeded in clearing a way through the strait, but then became trapped in the Sea of Marmora without any troops to occupy captured territory.:252 Churchill had anticipated the loss of ships: the battleships were mainly chosen because they were obsolete and unfit to face modern German ships, and he believed that the attack should have continued.:vol.2 670–690 Commodore Roger Keyes (Carden's chief of staff) believed that with destroyers fitted for minesweeping, and with naval personnel manning the trawlers, the mines could have been removed. These improvements were carried out, but never tried against the defences. It was also reported at the time that the defences were short of ammunition, and now seems likely that at least some of guns, particularly the largest, would have been forced to cease firing the following day.

The landings by the ANZAC, the 29th and Royal Naval divisions, and a French division were delayed until 25 April because of lack of preparations, by which time the Turks had deployed six divisions and created barbed wire and trench defences on likely landing sites. The landings failed. Churchill was widely blamed for the fiasco. He was probably right in saying that had the naval attacks been pressed the Turks, short of ammunition and low in morale would have had to abandon the forts and the Fleet could have occupied the Sea of Marmora and with it Constantinople.:165 But it is even more likely that had the Fleet been properly equipped with spotter planes and destroyer minesweepers, the attack on 18 March would have been successful. It is almost certain that a Fleet so equipped and supported by the four divisions made available in April would have cleared the Strait with almost no loss. As the minister responsible, Churchill was the one who did not provide the resources needed.:97–99 Clement Attlee, who served in the army at Gallipoli, described the campaign as "an immortal gamble that did not come off... Sir Winston had the one strategic idea in the war. He did not believe in throwing away masses of people to be massacred".:260

The Asquith Coalition, the Dardanelles Committee

The Liberal government was weakened by the failure of the naval attacks and the first landings in Gallipoli, by the failure of the offensive at Neuve Chapelle, and by the Shell Crisis. The Cabinet was bickering and some members plotted against others. Churchill himself aimed to replace Sir Edward Grey as Foreign Secretary with Balfour.:304 The historian Stephen Koss has argued that Churchill himself created the Shell Crisis. He states that during a visit to BEF Headquarters on 8 May he arranged with Colonel Charles à Court Repington, the Times correspondent there to publish the reports of the lack of shells. James discounts this argument.:184 On 15 May Fisher resigned as First Sea Lord. He presented the Cabinet with a list of demands; if these were satisfied he would return to office. The first of these was that Churchill would be dismissed from Cabinet altogether. Fisher's demands were extreme, the King saying that Fisher should be hung from the yardarm, but his resignation precipitated a Cabinet crisis.

Prime Minister Asquith formed an all-party coalition government. The Conservatives demanded Churchill's demotion as the price for entry.:282–288 He had little support in Cabinet or in the Liberal Party as a whole. Many thought the same as Lloyd George: that Churchill's ambition had led him to override his professional advisers and his record was a succession of grisly failures.:309 Others, including Mrs Asquith, blamed him for breaking the Cabinet and forcing the Coalition.

Churchill was demoted to the sinecure of Chancellor of the Duchy of Lancaster and became a member of the newly formed Dardanelles Committee. Churchill blamed Asquith for the demotion, but in fact Asquith and Lloyd George attempted to make Churchill Colonial Secretary.

In June and again in July, with Kitchener's support he argued for increased forces to be sent to Gallipoli. This led to the despatch of the 2nd Australian Division and the IX Corps to Gallipoli and to the landing at Suvla Bay. The attacks on Churchill redoubled when this landing failed. The Committee appointed General Sir Charles Monro as Commander. He advised evacuation. Churchill bitterly opposed this.:ch. XXXIII The Committee despatched Kitchener to report. He too advised evacuation. Before this took place, the Dardanelles Committee was replaced by a War Committee on 11 November. Churchill was not appointed to this Committee. On 15 November, Churchill resigned from his post, feeling his energies were not being used. During Churchill's time on the Dardanelles Committee he was the sole Liberal supporter of Lloyd George's campaign for conscription. This served to separate him further from the majority of the Liberal Party without healing his breach with the Conservatives, though many of them supported conscription.

Upon resigning he rejoined the army, though remaining an MP, and served for several months on the Western Front as commander of the 6th Battalion of the Royal Scots Fusiliers, with the rank of Lieutenant-Colonel. During this period, his second-in-command was a young Archibald Sinclair who later led the Liberal Party. Although Churchill did spend some time behind the front, visiting leaders such as Field Marshal Sir John French, Churchill led his battalion into the trenches on 27 January 1916.:301 In March, Churchill returned to Britain after he had become restless in France and wished to speak again in the House of Commons.:309 Sir Edward Carson encouraged him to do so.

Return to power

When he returned to Parliament in summer 1916 Churchill sat on the opposition benches. The opposition at this time was largely dissatisfied Conservatives who were not in the Coalition and was headed by Carson. This changed in December 1916, when Asquith resigned as Prime Minister being replaced by Lloyd George. From then on the opposition was largely the Liberal supporters of Asquith. Churchill was a member of neither group.:114–16:125–29 He was mainly occupied in giving evidence before the Dardanelles Commission, though at Balfour's request he wrote a semi-official statement on the

Battle of Jutland.

In July 1917, Churchill was appointed Minister of Munitions. For some months Lloyd George had feared that Churchill might challenge his leadership,:407 and after a masterly speech by Churchill in a secret session of the Commons on 10 May, Lloyd George approached him seeking his assistance.:130 The Conservatives and The Times objected to Lloyd George's first proposal - that Churchill be appointed to head the Air Board. Lloyd George then asked Beaverbrook to obtain Bonar Law's agreement to Churchill's appointment (which Lloyd George had already determined upon) to the Ministry of Munitions.:311 Bonar Law said correctly "Lloyd George's throne will shake." Churchill's own account mentions the important part Freddie Guest (then chief Coalition Liberal whip) played in this but does not disclose that Guest was Churchill's cousin.:1112 This episode, with its behind-the-scenes negotiations, shows how unpopular Churchill remained at this stage. As Minister, Churchill reorganised the department, arbitrated between the various services' demands for weapons, and repeated his advocacy for tanks, but most of his work was administering an already functioning department. He was a "competent, energetic, and efficient" minister.

Post-war coalition

In January 1919, after the 1918 Coupon election, Churchill

became Secretary of State for War and Secretary of State for Air. He was not a member of the War Cabinet, which continued until November 1919.:478–79 Churchill had pressed for appointment as Minister of Defence, combining all three service departments and the Ministry of Munitions (now renamed the Ministry of Supply and with a seat in Cabinet). He was unsuccessful.

His first challenge was demobilisation. He inherited a scheme whereby those men required most for industry would be demobilised first. In practise this meant that those who had served in the forces the shortest were being released from the forces first. Soldiers rioted, at one time burning Luton Town Hall. Churchill scrapped the system, instead releasing those who had served longest first.:130–32 The soldiers' unrest was but one domestic problem: there were strikes and riots in Glasgow, and a proposed national miners strike. Churchill suggested using four divisions of the Rhine Army as strikebreakers.

He was the main architect of the Ten Year Rule, a principle that allowed the Treasury to dominate and control strategic, foreign, and financial policies under the assumption that "there would be no great European war for the next five or ten years". He substantially reduced the RAF – so that it would have four Home and eighteen Imperial squadrons, and he rejected proposals for government support of civil aviation. Liddell Hart commented: "He was anxious to make a fresh start in current political affairs, and the best chance lay in the post-war retrenchment of expenditure."

A major preoccupation of his tenure in the War Office was the Allied intervention in the Russian Civil War. British forces were already in Russia, at Murmansk, in Siberia, and guarding the Baku railway before Churchill took charge at the War Office. The Cabinet was divided, without a clear policy. While Lloyd George proposed negotiations between all the Russian groups, which led to U.S. President Woodrow Wilson's abortive Prinkipo Plan, Red Army attacks on the British positions led the Cabinet to approve 'forward defence".:137

Churchill was a staunch advocate of foreign intervention, declaring that Bolshevism must be "strangled in its cradle". He secured, from a divided and loosely organised Cabinet,:143–150:495–519 intensification and prolongation of the British involvement beyond the wishes of any major group in Parliament or the nation – and in the face of the bitter hostility of the Labour Party. On 14 January 1919 Churchill circulated a Most urgent and secret memorandum to all commanders of British forces asking whether their forces would serve overseas and particularly in Russia, whether they would serve as strikebreakers and the soldiers' attitude to trade unions. A copy was leaked to and published in the Daily Herald.:139 In February he attempted to get American and then general Allied support for protracted large-scale intervention. In April he pushed for an offensive, rather than a defensive role for the North Russia force. Claiming the scheme was that of General Ironside and that it was essential for a subsequent evacuation, he wanted the force to link up with Admiral Aleksandr Kolchak's forces to the east.:502 In May after failing to get Cabinet approval to expand the British-Slavo Legion, he decided this was a purely War Office decision, expanded the Legion, and reported this to the Cabinet, which merely 'noted' the matter.:144 In July, when Kolchak's force was retreating rapidly, he told the cabinet that a White defeat would allow the Bolsheviks to threaten Poland, Romania, and Czechoslovakia.:152 From then until the final evacuation, Churchill continued to argue for support for the White forces. In 1920, after the last British forces had been withdrawn, Churchill was instrumental in having arms sent to the Poles when they invaded Ukraine.

Churchill's actions in supporting the White forces led to a break with Lloyd George which was never completely healed,:502–504:180–83:180–83 criticism by the Press:165 and further distrust from Labour.:158–59

Churchill was responsible for establishing both the Auxiliary Division and the Black and Tans during the Irish War of Independence. He defended their activities, saying they enjoyed the same freedom as police in Chicago or New York in dealing with armed gangs. He initially advocated the military defeat of the IRA and its supporters. By summer 1921, however, as the Colonial Secretary he was pressing for negotiations. His desired negotiating position was to offer a measure of Irish self-government from a position of strength: he "wished to couple a tremendous onslaught with the fairest offer."

In 1920, as Secretary of State for War and Air, Churchill was responsible for quelling rebellions in British Somaliland and the uprising of Kurds and Arabs in British-occupied

Mesopotamia. In each case the rebellions were crushed by co-ordinated air force and army operations. Churchill told the Commons that whereas an army campaign in Somalia would have cost £6,000,000 the air force expedition had cost £70,000. It had involved 6 Airco DH9 bombers and a total of less than 250 aircrew.

Colonial Secretary

Churchill became Secretary of State for the Colonies in 1921 and was a signatory of the Anglo-Irish Treaty of 1921, which established the Irish Free State. Churchill was involved in the lengthy negotiations of the treaty. To protect British maritime interests, he casued the agreement to include three Treaty Ports (Queenstown (Cobh), Berehaven, and Lough Swilly), which could be used as Atlantic bases by the Royal Navy.:361–365 (The bases were ceded to Ireland in 1938, under the terms of the Anglo-Irish Trade Agreement.) The Irish Civil War broke out after the signing of the Treaty, Churchill supported the government of the Free State with arms and ordered the British forces still in Ireland to assist the Irish National Army against the Republican Army. Churchill's other main concern while Colonial Secretary was the Middle East. He wanted Egypt (then administered by the Foreign Office) to be brought under his department's control.:174 He was faced with continuing riots and communal violence in those parts of the former Ottoman Empire that British forces occupied after World War I. Most of these riots were against the British occupation. Churchill did not want to give the complete independence that some of the Arabs had been promised. Rather, his aims were to reduce the British forces in the region and to ensure that British interests, particularly in the air route to India and the oil fields, were protected. The local population was a less important issue.

After setting up a Middle Eastern Department within the Colonial Office, Churchill convened a conference in Cairo in March 1921, attended by T. E. Lawrence, Gertrude Bell, Sir Hugh Trenchard, Sir John Salmond, and Sir Percy Cox. No Arabs were invited to the conference.

The method recommended by the Conference and chosen by Churchill, summarised by Sir Henry Wilson as 'hot air aeroplanes and Arabs', was the creation of the Kingdom of Iraq with Lawrence's friend Faisal as King, and the Emirate of Transjordan with Faisal's brother Abdullah as Emir. The boundaries of the two countries were joined in what is sometimes known as Winston's Hiccup. This was intentionally designed to ensure that the air route to India passed over the areas controlled by or friendly to Britain.

Churchill's creation of Iraq from three the Ottoman Vilayets of Basra, Baghdad, and Mosul has been criticised as making an artificial state which inevitably would break down. He has also been criticised for advocating the use of gas as a weapon against Arab and Kurdish 'insurgents'. His defenders show that what he intended was the use of generally non-lethal (tear) gas, but those gases were known to kill children and the ill. His policy was to control Iraq with the minimum expenses, so he refused to authorise such projects as a hospital in Iraq.:239

In October 1922, Churchill underwent an operation to remove his appendix. While he was still in hospital, Lloyd George resigned as prime minister with a general election to be held on 15 November. Churchill was not sufficiently well to travel to his constituency in Dundee until 11 November, causing him great difficulties campaigning. Once there he was still not sufficiently well to stand to address an audience, but had to address meetings where he was heckled and unable to finish speaking. Clementine travelled to the constituency earlier with other friends, but generally the campaign was poorly managed in Churchill's absence.

The constituency had a significantly working-class composition, so that his principal opponents were a candidate for the steadily rising Labour Party, E. D. Morel, and a local prohibitionist, Edwin Scrymgeour, who had stood unsuccessfully in the constituency many times, but steadily increasing his vote each time. The Dundee constituency returned two members, so Scrymgeour and Morel worked in partnership, each lending his factional support to the other. Churchill was partnered by another National Liberal, but they were opposed by an Asquithian Liberal candidate following the split in the party. The result was that Scrymgeour and Morel won, with Churchill relegated to fourth place behind his running mate.:370–375 Churchill quipped later that he left Dundee "without an office, without a seat, without a party, and without an appendix". The result of the general election was the first non-coalition Conservative government since 1900. The Liberal Party never recovered the position in politics which it had once enjoyed.

Churchill stood for the Liberals again in the 1923 general election, losing in Leicester, but over the next few months he moved towards the Conservative Party in all but name. His first electoral contest as an independent candidate, fought under the label of "Independent Anti-Socialist", was a narrow loss in a by-election in the Westminster Abbey constituency – his third electoral defeat in fewer than two years. However, he stood for election yet again several months later in the general election of 1924, again as an independent candidate, this time under the label of "Constitutionalist" although with Conservative backing, and was finally elected to represent Epping. The following year, he formally rejoined the Conservative Party, commenting wryly that "Anyone can rat, but it takes a certain ingenuity to re-rat."

Chancellor of the Exchequer

Churchill was appointed Chancellor of the Exchequer in 1924 under Stanley Baldwin and oversaw Britain's disastrous return to the gold standard, which resulted in deflation, unemployment, and the miners' strike that led to the General Strike of 1926. His decision, announced in the 1924 budget, came after long consultation with treasury officials, various economists, and the board of the Bank of England. Churchill was sceptical about the benefits of returning to the gold standard, and widely questioned the almost unanimous advice he was receiving that it was necessary. The governor of the Bank of England, Montagu Norman, said that 'there was no alternative to a return to gold'. The permanent secretary to the treasury, Sir Otto Niemeyer said that not to do so would show

Britain had never 'meant business' about the gold standard, and that 'our nerve had failed'. The parliamentary joint select committee on Currency and Banking under its chairman Lord Bradbury (former permanent secretary to the treasury) supported a return, as did the Labour shadow chancellor, Snowden.:398–399

Churchill held a dinner at which the principal opponents of a return, economist John Maynard Keynes and former chancellor and chairman of the Midland Bank Reginald McKenna, were encouraged to argue out their case with Niemeyer and Bradbury. The dinner continued into the early hours of the morning but, in the end, Keynes's academic arguments proved unconvincing, and McKenna conceded that Churchill had little political choice except to return to gold.:400 This decision later prompted Keynes to write The Economic Consequences of Mr. Churchill, arguing that the return to the gold standard at the pre-war parity in 1925 ($£1=\$4.86$) would lead to a world depression. Interestingly, the pamphlet did not criticise the decision to return to the gold standard per se. The decision was generally popular and seen as 'sound economics' although it was opposed by Lord Beaverbrook and the Federation of British Industries.:207

Churchill later regarded this as the greatest mistake of his life; in discussions with McKenna, he acknowledged that the return to the gold standard and the resulting 'dear money' policy was economically bad. In those discussions, he maintained the policy as fundamentally political—a return to the pre-war conditions in which he believed.:206 In his speech on the bill he said "I will tell you what it the return to the gold standard will shackle us to. It will shackle us to reality." Writing about the events in his biography of Churchill, Roy Jenkins argued that, although Churchill had challenged the proposal to return to the gold standard in the face of almost unanimous political and institutional support, he had been the only person who could have prevented the return to gold and its consequences, so responsibility remained with him for the decision.:401

The return to the pre-war exchange rate and to the gold standard depressed industries, the most affected being coal mining. Already suffering from declining output as shipping switched to oil, and basic British industries like cotton came under more competition in export markets, the return to the pre-war exchange was estimated to add up to 10% in costs to the industry. In July 1925 a commission of inquiry reported generally favouring the miners', rather than the mine owners' position.:405 Attached to the report was a memorandum from Sir Josiah Stamp stating that the increased difficulties in the coal industry could be entirely explained by the "immediate and necessary effects of the return to gold".Baldwin, with Churchill's support, proposed a subsidy to the industry while a royal commission prepared a further report. During the general strike of 1926, Churchill was reported to have suggested that machine guns be used on the striking miners. Churchill edited the government's newspaper, the British Gazette, and, during the dispute, he argued that "either the country will break the general strike, or the general strike will break the country." Furthermore, he controversially claimed that the fascism of Benito Mussolini had "rendered a service to the whole world,"

showing, as it had, "a way to combat subversive forces" —
that is, he considered Mussolini's regime to be a bulwark against
the perceived threat of Communist revolution. At one point,
Churchill went as far as to call Mussolini the "Roman genius...
the greatest lawgiver among men.":78

It was not only the return to the gold standard that later
economists, as well as those at the time, criticised in Churchill's
time at the treasury. Rather it was his budget measures which,
even given the consensus at the time that the budgets should
be balanced, were attacked as assisting the generally prosperous
rentier banking and salaried classes (to which Churchill and
his associates generally belonged) at the expense of
manufacturers and exporters which were known then to be
suffering from imports and from competition in traditional
export markets. However his 1925 budget was well received
by the public and enhanced Churchill's prestige.:404 Churchill
had served in two of the four Great Offices of State and several
other positions, no one had more experience in government,
and he could expect another high office in the next
Conservative ministry.

Political Isolation

The Conservative government was defeated in the 1929
General Election. Churchill did not seek election to the
Conservative Business Committee, the official leadership of

the Conservative MPs. Over the next two years, Churchill became estranged from the Conservative leadership over the issues of protective tariffs and Indian Home Rule, which he bitterly opposed. He further distanced himself from the party as a whole by his political views and by his friendships with press barons, financiers, and people whose characters were seen as dubious. When Ramsay MacDonald formed the National Government in 1931, Churchill was not invited to join the Cabinet. He was at the low point in his career, in a period known as "the wilderness years". He spent much of the next few years concentrating on his writing, including Marlborough: His Life and Times – a biography of his ancestor John Churchill, 1st Duke of Marlborough – and A History of the English Speaking Peoples (though the latter was not published until well after World War II). Churchill's depiction of Marlborough in Marlborough: His Life and Times had shown close parallels to his own stand against appeasement. Both were war leaders advocating firm policies, but surrounded by an attacking public and hostile politicians.:402:395–400 In doing so they echo public comments at the time. The Daily Express referred to Churchill's speech in October 1938 against the Munich agreement as "an alarmist oration by a man whose mind is soaked in the conquests of Marlborough".

Though badly hurt when he was struck by a car in New York City on a North American speaking tour, he wrote a profitable article about the experience. He wrote many other articles, collections of speeches, and several books - some such as his Great Contemporaries of lasting worth. He supported himself largely by his writing and was one of the best paid writers of his time.

Nevertheless, he was still in financial difficulties, having lost most of his American investments in the Wall Street Crash. He was criticised for holidaying in the Riviera and America as the guest of such people as Beaverbrook amd William Randolph Hearst, and for drinking and gambling with people such as Brendan Bracken and, until his early death, Lord Birkenhead.:31–36 These attacks were not new; in 1922 Churchill had brought a successful libel action against Lord Alfred Douglas who had accused Churchill of giving a deliberately false account of the Battle of Jutland at the request of Sir Ernest Cassel. During the trial it emerged that Cassell, whose company remained Churchill's publisher, had paid for some of the furnishings of Churchill's London residence.

His political views, set forth in his 1930 Romanes Election and published as Parliamentary Government and the Economic Problem (republished in 1932 in his collection of essays "Thoughts and Adventures") involved abandoning universal suffrage, a return to a property franchise, proportional representation for the major cities, and an economic 'sub-parliament'.

Indian Independence

During the first half of the 1930s, outspoken opposition

towards the granting of Dominion status to India became one of Churchill's major political focuses. Churchill was one of the founders of the India Defence League, a group dedicated to the preservation of British power in India. In speeches and press articles in this period, he forecast widespread British unemployment and civil strife in India should independence be granted.:260 The Viceroy, Lord Irwin, who had been appointed by the prior Conservative Government, engaged in the Round Table Conference in early 1931 and then announced the Government's policy that India should be granted Dominion Status. In this the Government was supported by the Liberal Party and, officially at least, by the Conservative Party.

Churchill denounced the Round Table Conference. He spoke at public meetings in Manchester and Liverpool in January and February 1931, respectively. At both he forecast widespread unemployment into the millions and other social and economic problems in the United Kingdom if India became self-governing.:259 Though he would come to respect Mohandas Gandhi, especially after Gandhi "stood up for the untouchables",:618 at a meeting of the West Essex Conservative Association specially convened so Churchill could explain his position he said, "It is alarming and also nauseating to see Mr Gandhi, a seditious Middle-Temple lawyer, now posing as a fakir of a type well-known in the East, striding half-naked up the steps of the Vice-regal palace... to parley on equal terms with the representative of the King-Emperor.":390 He called the Indian Congress leaders "Brahmins who mouth and patter principles of Western Liberalism."

In Parliament on 26 January 1931, he attacked the Government's policy, saying that the Round Table Conference "was a frightful prospect" and that he would support "effective and real organisms of provisional and local government in the provinces." He returned to the Parliamentary attack on 13 March. Baldwin answered him by quoting Churchill's own speech in winding up the debate for the Lloyd George Coalition government on Amritsar massacre, in which Churchill defended the cashiering of General Reginald Dyer. Baldwin continued by challenging Churchill and his other critics to depose him as leader of the Conservative Party.

There were two incidents which damaged Churchill's reputation greatly within the Conservative Party in the period. Both were seen at the time as attacks on the Conservative leadership and as an attempt to undermine those Conservatives - and Baldwin in particular - who supported granting Dominion status to India.

The first was his speech on the eve of the St George by-election in April 1931. In a secure Conservative seat, official Conservative candidate Duff Cooper was opposed by an independent Conservative. The independent was supported by Lord Rothermere, Lord Beaverbrook, and their respective newspapers. Both press barons had tried to urge specific policies on the Conservative Party: Rothermere opposed Indian home rule, and Beaverbrook pressed for tariff reform under the slogan Empire Free Trade. Churchill's speech at the Albert Hall had been arranged before the date of the by-election had been set.:262 But he made no attempt to change the date and his speech was seen as a part of the press barons' campaign against Baldwin. This was reinforced by Churchill's personal friendship with both, but especially with Beaverbrook, who wrote "The primary issue of the by-election will be the leadership of the Conservative Party. If... (the independent candidate wins) Baldwin must go.":304 Baldwin's position was strengthened when Duff Cooper won and when the civil disobedience campaign in India ceased with the Gandhi-Irwin Pact.

The second issue also affected Churchill's reputation. On 16 April 1934 Churchill claimed in Parliament that Sir Samuel Hoare and Lord Derby had pressured the Manchester Chamber of Commerce to change evidence it had given to the Joint Select Committee considering the Government of India Bill in June 1933. On 18 April he successfully moved that the matter be referred to the House of Commons Privilege Committee. He tried to cross-examine witnesses before the Committee, contrary to normal procedure. Churchill himself gave evidence and Austen Chamberlain criticised the manner in which he gave it. Churchill's evidence was little and the inquiry reported to the House that there had been no breach.:269–272 The report was debated on 13 June. Churchill was unable to find a single supporter in the House and the debate ended without a division. Leo Amery accused him of pressing the matter to bring the government down stating "at all costs he had to be faithful to his chosen motto: ;'Fiat justicia, ruat caelum." Churchill responded "Translate it!" Amery then remarked "I will translate it into the vernacular: 'If I can trip up Sam Hoare the government's bust'."

Churchill permanently broke with Stanley Baldwin over Indian independence and did not again hold any office while Baldwin was Prime Minister. In the index to The Gathering Storm, Churchill's first volume of his history of World War II, he records Baldwin "admitting to putting party before country" for his alleged admission that he would not have won the 1935 Election if he had pursued a more aggressive policy of rearmament.:343 Churchill selectively quotes a speech in the Commons by Baldwin and gives the false impression that Baldwin is speaking of the general election when he was speaking of a by-election in 1933, and omits altogether Baldwin's actual comments about the 1935 election: "we got from the country, a mandate for doing a thing a substantial rearmament programme that no one, twelve months before, would have believed possible." This canard had been first put forward in the first edition of Guilty Men but in subsequent editions (including those before Churchill wrote The Gathering Storm) had been corrected.

Churchill continued his campaign against any further transfer of power to Indian natives. He continued to predict conflict in India and mass unemployment at home. His speeches often quoted nineteenth-century politicians and his own policy was to maintain the existing Raj. In pursuing this campaign Churchill cut himself off from the mainstream of Conservative politics as much as from the rest of the political world. Younger Conservatives such as Duff Cooper, who later described Churchill's campaign as the most unfortunate event that occurred between the two wars, and Harold Macmillan saw Churchill as a reactionary, someone who was completely out of touch and at base, undemocratic - leaning towards the totalitarian regimes. Churchill's public comments often seemed that way.

Some historians see his basic attitude to India as being set out in his book My Early Life (1930) and as being unchanged since his military service before he entered parliament. In so saying they note his references in his speeches on India to late Victorian politicians such as John Morley.:258 Historians also dispute his motives in maintaining his opposition. Some see him as trying to destabilise the National Government. In this they follow Amery (see above) and Lloyd George, who believed that with MacDonald ill and Churchill leading the Conservative right-wing, Baldwin would have to form a new Coalition in which both he and Churchill would have had key ministries. Some historians also draw a parallel between Churchill's attitudes to India and those towards the Nazis.

German rearmament

Churchill was wary of Adolf Hitler's potential danger as early as 1930. More than two years before Hitler took power in January 1933, Churchill warned at a dinner at the German Embassy that Hitler and his followers would start a war as soon as possible. Beginning in 1932, when he opposed those who advocated giving Germany the right to military parity with France, Churchill spoke often of the dangers of German rearmament.:285–86 Later, particularly in The Gathering Storm, he tried to portray himself as being for a time, a lone voice calling on Britain to strengthen itself against Germany.:75

However Lord Lloyd was the first to so agitate. Churchill also tried to portray himself as warning against German rearmament as early as 1930 and as opposing what he saw as British disarmament at and before that time. He omits the fact that as Chancellor of the Exchequer he had imposed the heavy defence cuts referred to above.

Churchill's attitude toward fascist (and quasi-fascist) rulers was ambiguous. In 1931 he warned against the League of Nations opposing the Japanese in Manchuria: "I hope we shall try in England to understand the position of Japan an ancient state.... On the one side they have the dark menace of Soviet Russia. On the other the chaos of China four or five provinces of which are being tortured under Communist rule".:329 In contemporary newspaper articles he referred to the Spanish Republican government as a Communist front, and Franco's army as the "Anti red movement" and writing "revivified Fascist Spain in closest sympathy with Italy and Germany is one kind of disaster. A Communist Spain reaching its snaky tentacles through Portugal and France is another, and many will think the worse.":408 He supported the Hoare-Laval Pact and continued up until 1937 to praise Benito Mussolini.:375 In his 1937 book Great Contemporaries, Churchill expressed a hope that despite Hitler's apparent dictatorial tendencies, he would use his power to rebuild Germany into a worthy member of the world community.

Churchill's first major speech on defence on 7 February 1934 stressed the need to rebuild the Royal Air Force and to create a Ministry of Defence; his second, on 13 July, urged a renewed role for the League of Nations. These three topics remained his themes until early 1936. In 1935 he was one of the founding members of "Focus", a group which also included Sir Archibald Sinclair, Lady Violet Bonham Carter, Wickham Steed, and Professor Gilbert Murray. Focus brought together people of differing political backgrounds and occupations who were united in seeking 'the defence of freedom and peace'. Focus led to the formation of the much wider Arms and the Covenant Movement in 1936. When the Germany reoccupied the Rhineland in February 1936, Churchill was holidaying in Spain, and returned to a divided Britain. Labour opposition was adamant in opposing sanctions and the National Government was divided between advocates of economic sanctions and those who said that even these would lead to a humiliating backdown by Britain, as France would not support any intervention. Churchill's speech on 9 March was measured and praised by Neville Chamberlain as constructive. But within weeks Churchill was passed over for the post of Minister for Co-ordination of Defence in favour of the Attorney General, Sir Thomas Inskip.

This surprising appointment—it surprised Inskip as much as anyone, and A. J. P. Taylor later wrote of "an appointment rightly described as the most extraordinary since Caligula made his horse a consul"—came despite advice to Baldwin to broaden his cabinet. Historians have variously seen it as Baldwin's caution in not wanting to appoint someone as controversial as Churchill, as avoiding giving Germany any sign that the United Kingdom was preparing for war, and as avoiding someone who had few allies in the Conservative Party and was opposed as a war monger by some people in the United Kingdom. Whatever the reason, it was a severe blow to Churchill.

In June 1936 Churchill organised a deputation of senior Conservatives who shared his concern to see Baldwin, Chamberlain, and Halifax. He had tried to include delegates from the other two parties, and later wrote "If the leaders of the Labour and Liberal oppositions had come with us there might have been a political situation so intense as to enforce remedial action.":276 As it was the meeting achieved little, Baldwin arguing that the Government was doing all it could given the anti-war feeling of the electorate. But it showed that more Conservatives shared Churchill's views—he was less isolated then he had been earlier. John Gunther wrote that year that he "may still become prime minister ... Churchill's judgment is faulty, people say; he is too impetuous and 'unstable'; but most people agree that in a great upheaval he would emerge as Britain's national leader."

Abdication Crisis

In June 1936, Walter Monckton told Churchill that the rumours that King Edward VIII intended to marry Mrs Wallis Simpson were true. Churchill then advised against the marriage and said he regarded Mrs Simpson's existing marriage as a 'safeguard'. In November he declined Lord Salisbury's invitation to be part of a delegation of senior Conservative backbenchers which met with Baldwin to discuss the matter. On 25 November he, Clement Attlee, and Sinclair met with Baldwin and were told officially of the King's intention and asked whether they would form an administration if Baldwin and the National Government resigned should the King not take the Ministry's advice. Both Attlee and Sinclair said they would not take office if invited to do so. Churchill's reply was that his attitude was a little different but he would support the government. One reason why Churchill was invited to a meeting otherwise attended only by the leaders of the three political parties was that at the time of the Crisis Churchill was seen as an alternative leader. As Lord Beaverbrook wrote "he has emerged as a leader of a big armaments anti-German movement in politics, hostile to the Government".:372

The abdication crisis became public in the first fortnight of December 1936. At this time Churchill publicly gave his support to the King. The first public meeting of the Arms and the Covenant Movement was on 3 December. Churchill was a major speaker and later wrote that in replying to the Vote of Thanks, he made a declaration 'on the spur of the moment' asking for delay before any decision was made by either the King or his Cabinet.:170–71 Others including Citrine, who chaired the meeting, wrote that Churchill did not make such a speech. Later that night, Churchill saw the draft of the King's proposed wireless broadcast, and spoke with Beaverbrook and the King's solicitor about it.

On 4 December, he met with the King and again urged delay in any decision about abdication. On 5 December, he issued a lengthy statement implying that the Ministry was applying unconstitutional pressure on the King to force him to make a hasty decision.:349–351 On 7 December, he tried to address the Commons to plead for delay. He was shouted down. Seemingly staggered by the unanimous hostility of all Members, he left. Churchill's reputation in Parliament and the United Kingdom as a whole was badly damaged. Some such as Alistair Cooke saw him as trying to build a King's Party. Others like Harold Macmillan were dismayed by the damage Churchill's support for the King had done to the Arms and the Covenant Movement. Churchill himself later wrote "I was myself smitten in public opinion that it was the almost universal view that my political life was ended." One unresolved issue is the amount of Churchill's involvement with the King's address, the first draft of which the Cabinet refused to let the King air - it was rightly said to be the King seeking to appeal to the people against the Ministry. The King (by then Duke of Windsor) acknowledged Churchill's help in writing the speech, but some historians say that Churchill wrote it all.

Historians are divided about Churchill's motives in his support for Edward VIII. Some, such as A.J.P. Taylor, see it as being an attempt to 'overthrow the government of feeble men'. Others, such as James, see Churchill's motives as entirely honourable and disinterested, indicating that he felt deeply for the King.

Return from exile

Churchill later sought to portray himself as an isolated voice warning of the need to rearm against Germany. While it is true that he had little following in the House of Commons during much of the 1930s, he was given considerable privileges by the government. The "Churchill group" in the latter half of the decade consisted only of him, Duncan Sandys, and Brendan Bracken. It was isolated from the other main factions within the Conservative Party pressing for faster rearmament and a stronger foreign policy. In some senses the 'exile' was more apparent then real. Churchill continued to be consulted on many matters by the government or seen as an alternative leader.

Even while Churchill was campaigning against Indian independence, he received official and otherwise secret information. From 1932, Churchill's neighbour, Major Desmond Morton, with Ramsay MacDonald's approval, gave Churchill information on German air power.:302 From 1930 onwards Morton headed a department of the Committee of Imperial Defence charged with researching the defence preparedness of other nations. Lord Swinton, the Secretary of State for Air, with Baldwin's approval in 1934 gave Churchill access to official and otherwise secret information. Swinton did so, knowing Churchill would remain a critic of the government but believing that an informed critic was better than one relying on rumour and hearsay.

When Chamberlain replaced Baldwin as prime minister in May 1937 he did not bring Churchill into the government; besides the appeasement issue, Chamberlain told Churchill supporter Leslie Hore-Belisha that "if I take him into the Cabinet he will dominate it. He won't give others the chance of even talking." Churchill was a fierce critic of Neville Chamberlain's appeasement of Hitler:149–150 and in private letters to Lloyd George (13 August) and Lord Moyne (11 September) just before the Munich Agreement, he wrote that the government was faced with a choice between "war and shame" and that, having chosen shame, would later get war on less favourable terms. Churchill's reputation was probably at its lowest point in 1937-1938, but by 1939, after Germany had absorbed Austria and conquered Czechoslovakia, he was seen as having been proven right. When Germany invaded Poland in September 1939, Chamberlain appointed Churchill to the Cabinet as the First Lord of the Admiralty.

FIRST TERM AS PRIME MINISTER & WORLD WAR 2

On 3 September 1939, the day Britain declared war on Germany following the outbreak of the Second World War, Churchill was appointed First Lord of the Admiralty, the same position he had held during the first part of the First World War. As such he was a member of Chamberlain's small War Cabinet.

In this position, he proved to be one of the highest-profile ministers during the so-called "Phoney War," when the only noticeable action was at sea and the USSR's attack on Finland. Churchill advocated the pre-emptive occupation of the neutral Norwegian iron-ore port of Narvik and the iron mines in Kiruna, Sweden, early in the war. However, Chamberlain and the rest of the War Cabinet disagreed, and the operation was delayed until the successful German invasion of Norway. On 10 May 1940, hours before the German invasion of France by a lightning advance through the Low Countries, it became clear that, following failure in Norway, the country had no confidence in Chamberlain's prosecution of the war and so Chamberlain resigned. The commonly accepted version of events states that Lord Halifax turned down the post of prime minister because he believed he could not govern effectively as a member of the House of Lords instead of the House of Commons. Although the prime minister does not traditionally advise the King on the former's successor, Chamberlain wanted someone who would command the support of all three major parties in the House of Commons. A meeting between Chamberlain, Halifax, Churchill and David Margesson, the government Chief Whip, led to the recommendation of Churchill, and, as constitutional monarch, George VI asked Churchill to be prime minister. Churchill's first act was to write to Chamberlain to thank him for his support.

In June 1940, to encourage the neutral Irish state to join with the Allies, Churchill indicated to the Taoiseach Éamon de Valera that the United Kingdom would push for Irish unity, but believing that Churchill could not deliver, de Valera declined the offer. The British did not inform the Government of Northern Ireland that they had made the offer to the Dublin government, and De Valera's rejection was not publicised until 1970.

Churchill was still unpopular among many Conservatives and the Establishment, who opposed his replacing Chamberlain; the former prime minister remained party leader until dying in November. Churchill probably could not have won a majority in any of the political parties in the House of Commons, and the House of Lords was completely silent when it learned of his appointment. An American visitor reported in late 1940 that, "Everywhere I went in London people admired Churchill's energy, his courage, his singleness of purpose.

People said they didn't know what Britain would do without him. He was obviously respected. But no one felt he would be Prime Minister after the war. He was simply the right man in the right job at the right time. The time being the time of a desperate war with Britain's enemies."

An element of British public and political sentiment favoured a negotiated peace with Germany, among them Halifax as Foreign Secretary, but Churchill refused to consider an armistice. Although at times personally pessimistic about Britain's chances for victory—Churchill told Hastings Ismay on 12 June 1940 that "you and I will be dead in three months' time"—his use of rhetoric hardened public opinion against a peaceful resolution and prepared the British for a long war. Coining the general term for the upcoming battle, Churchill stated in his "finest hour" speech to the House of Commons on 18 June, "I expect that the Battle of Britain is about to begin." By refusing an armistice with Germany, Churchill kept resistance alive in the British Empire and created the basis for the later Allied counter-attacks of 1942–45, with Britain serving as a platform for the supply of the Soviet Union and the liberation of Western Europe.

In response to previous criticisms that there had been no clear single minister in charge of the prosecution of the war Churchill created and took the additional position of Minister of Defence, making him the most powerful wartime prime minister in British history. He immediately put his friend and confidant, industrialist and newspaper baron Lord Beaverbrook, in charge of aircraft production. It was Beaverbrook's business acumen that allowed Britain to quickly gear up aircraft production and engineering, which eventually made the difference in the war.

The war energised Churchill, who was 65 years old when he became Prime Minister. An American journalist wrote in 1941: "The responsibilities which are his now must be greater than those carried by any other human being on earth. One would think such a weight would have a crushing effect upon him. Not at all. The last time I saw him, while the Battle of Britain was still raging, he looked twenty years younger than before the war began ... His uplifted spirit is transmitted to the people". Churchill's speeches were a great inspiration to the embattled British. His first as prime minister was the famous, "I have nothing to offer but blood, toil, tears, and sweat" speech. One historian has called its effect on Parliament as "electrifying". The House of Commons that had ignored him during the 1930s "was now listening, and cheering". Churchill followed that closely with two other equally famous ones, given just before the Battle of Britain.

At the height of the Battle of Britain, his bracing survey of the situation included the memorable line "Never in the field of human conflict was so much owed by so many to so few", which engendered the enduring nickname The Few for the RAF fighter pilots who won it. He first spoke these famous words upon his exit from No. 11 Group's underground bunker at RAF Uxbridge, now known as the Battle of Britain Bunker on 16 August 1940. One of his most memorable war speeches came on 10 November 1942 at the Lord Mayor's Luncheon at

Mansion House in London, in response to the Allied victory at the Second Battle of El Alamein. Churchill stated:

"This is not the end. It is not even the beginning of the end. But it is, perhaps, the end of the beginning."

Without having much in the way of sustenance or good news to offer the British people, he took a risk in deliberately choosing to emphasise the dangers instead.

"Rhetorical power", wrote Churchill, "is neither wholly bestowed, nor wholly acquired, but cultivated." Not all were impressed by his oratory. Robert Menzies, prime minister of Australia and himself a gifted phrase-maker, said of Churchill during the Second World War: "His real tyrant is the glittering phrase so attractive to his mind that awkward facts have to give way." Another associate wrote: "He is ... the slave of the words which his mind forms about ideas ... And he can convince himself of almost every truth if it is once allowed thus to start on its wild career through his rhetorical machinery."

Since the appearance in 1966 of Lord Moran's memoir of his years as Churchill's doctor, with its claim that "Black Dog" was the name Churchill gave to "the prolonged fits of depression from which he suffered", many authors have suggested that throughout his life Churchill was a victim of, or at risk from, clinical depression. Formulated in this way, Churchill's mental health history contains unmistakable echoes of the seminal interpretation of Lord Moran's Black Dog revelations made by Dr Anthony Storr. In drawing so heavily on Moran for what he took to be the latter's totally reliable, first-hand clinical evidence of Churchill's lifelong struggle with "prolonged and recurrent depression" and its associated "despair", Storr produced a seemingly authoritative and persuasive diagnostic essay that, in the words of John Ramsden, "strongly influenced all later accounts."

However, Storr was not aware that, as Moran's biographer Professor Richard Lovell has shown, Moran, contrary to the impression created in his book, kept no diary, in the dictionary sense of the word, during his years as Churchill's doctor. Nor was Storr aware that Moran's book as published was a much rewritten account which mixed together Moran's contemporaneous jottings with later material acquired from other sources. As Wilfred Attenborough has demonstrated, the key Black Dog 'diary' entry for 14 August 1944 was an arbitrarily dated pastiche in which the explicit reference to Black Dog— the first of the few in the book (with an associated footnote definition of the term)—was taken, not from anything Churchill had said to Moran, but from much later claims made to Moran by Brendan Bracken (a non-clinician, of course) in 1958. Although seemingly unnoticed by Dr Storr and those he influenced, Moran later on in his book retracts his earlier suggestion, also derived from Brendan Bracken, that, towards the end of the Second World War, Churchill was succumbing to "the inborn melancholia of the Churchill blood"; also unnoticed by Storr et al., Moran, in his final chapter, states that Churchill, before the start of the First World War, "had managed to extirpate bouts of depression from his system".

Despite the difficulties with Moran's book, the many illustrations it provides of a Churchill understandably plunged into temporary low mood by military defeats and other severely adverse developments constitute a compelling portrait of a great man reacting to, but not significantly impeded by, worry and overstrain, a compelling portrait that is entirely consistent with the portraits of others who worked closely with Churchill. Moreover, it can be readily deduced from Moran's book that Churchill did not receive medication for depression – the amphetamine that Moran prescribed for special occasions, especially for big speeches from the autumn of 1953 onwards, was to combat the effects of Churchill's stroke of that year.

Churchill himself seems, in a long life, to have written about Black Dog on one occasion only: the reference, a backward-looking one, occurs in a private handwritten letter to Clementine Churchill dated July 1911 which reports the successful treatment of a relative's depression by a doctor in Germany. His ministerial circumstances at that date, the very limited treatments available for serious depression pre-1911, the fact of the relative's being "complete cured", and, not least, the evident deep interest Churchill took in the fact of the complete cure, can be shown to point to Churchill's pre-1911 Black Dog depression's having been a form of mild (i.e. non-psychotic) anxiety-depression, as that term is defined by Professor Edward Shorter.

It will be apparent from the preceding paragraphs that there is a serious doubt about the reliability of the evidential foundations of the dominant, essentially Storrian, perception that Churchill's mental health was an open-and-shut case of clinical depression. Moran himself leaned strongly in the direction of his patient's being "by nature very apprehensive"; close associates of Churchill have disputed the idea that apprehension was a defining feature of Churchill's temperament, although they readily concede that he was noticeably worried and anxious about some matters, especially in the buildup to important speeches in the House of Commons and elsewhere. And Churchill himself all but openly acknowledged in his book 'Painting as a Pastime' that he was prey to the "worry and mental overstrain experienced by persons who, over prolonged periods, have to bear exceptional responsibilities and discharge duties upon a very large scale". The fact that he found a remedy in painting and bricklaying is a strong indicator that the condition as he defined it did not amount to 'clinical depression', certainly not as that term was understood during the lifetimes of himself and Lord Moran.

According to Lord Moran, during the war years Churchill sought solace in his tumbler of whisky and soda and his cigar. Churchill was also a very emotional man, unafraid to shed tears when appropriate. During some of his broadcast speeches it was noticed that he was trying to hold back the tears. Nevertheless, although the fall of Tobruk was, by Churchill's own account "one of the heaviest blows" he received during the war, there seem to have been no tears. Certainly, the next day Moran found him animated and vigorous. Field Marshal Alanbrooke, Chief of the Imperial General Staff, who had been present when President Roosevelt broke the news of the tragedy to Churchill, focused afterwards in his diary on the superbly well judged manner in which the President made his offer of immediate military assistance, despite Alanbrooke's being ever ready to highlight what he perceived to be Churchill's contradictory motivations and flawed character during the war.

Churchill's physical health became more fragile during the war, as shown by a mild heart attack he suffered in December 1941 at the White House and also in December 1943 when he contracted pneumonia. Despite this, he travelled over 100,000 miles (160,000 km) throughout the war to meet other national leaders. For security, he usually travelled using the alias Colonel Warden.

Relations with the United States

Churchill's good relationship with U.S. President Franklin D. Roosevelt—between 1939 and 1945 they exchanged an estimated 1,700 letters and telegrams and met 11 times; Churchill estimated that they had 120 days of close personal contact—helped secure vital food, oil and munitions via the North Atlantic shipping routes. It was for this reason that Churchill was relieved when Roosevelt was re-elected in 1940. Upon re-election, Roosevelt immediately set about implementing a new method of providing military hardware and shipping to Britain without the need for monetary payment. Roosevelt persuaded Congress that repayment for this immensely costly service would take the form of defending the US; and so Lend-Lease was born. Churchill had 12 strategic conferences with Roosevelt which covered the Atlantic Charter, Europe first strategy, the Declaration by the United

Nations and other war policies. After Pearl Harbor was attacked, Churchill's first thought in anticipation of US help was, "We have won the war!" On 26 December 1941, Churchill addressed a joint meeting of the US Congress, asking of Germany and Japan, "What kind of people do they think we are?" Churchill initiated the Special Operations Executive (SOE) under Hugh Dalton's Ministry of Economic Warfare, which established, conducted and fostered covert, subversive and partisan operations in occupied territories with notable success; and also the Commandos which established the pattern for most of the world's current Special Forces. The Russians referred to him as the "British Bulldog".

Churchill was party to treaties that would redraw post-Second World War European and Asian boundaries. These were discussed as early as 1943. At the Second Quebec Conference in 1944 he drafted and, together with Roosevelt, signed a less-harsh version of the original Morgenthau Plan, in which they pledged to convert Germany after its unconditional surrender "into a country primarily agricultural and pastoral in its character." Proposals for European boundaries and settlements were officially agreed to by President Harry S. Truman, Churchill, and Joseph Stalin at Potsdam. Churchill's strong relationship with Harry Truman was also of great significance to both countries. While he clearly regretted the loss of his close friend and counterpart Roosevelt, Churchill was enormously supportive of Truman in his first days in office, calling him, "the type of leader the world needs when it needs him most."

Relations with the Soviet Union

When Hitler invaded the Soviet Union, Winston Churchill, a vehement anti-communist, famously stated "If Hitler invaded Hell, I would at least make a favourable reference to the Devil in the House of Commons," regarding his policy toward Stalin. Soon, British supplies and tanks were flowing to help the Soviet Union.

The Casablanca Conference, a meeting of Allied powers held in Casablanca, Morocco, on 14 January through 23 January 1943, produced what was to be known as the "Casablanca Declaration". In attendance were Churchill, Franklin Roosevelt and Charles de Gaulle. Joseph Stalin had bowed out, citing the need for his presence in the Soviet Union to attend to the Stalingrad crisis. It was in Casablanca that the Allies made a unified commitment to continue the war through to the "unconditional surrender" of the Axis powers. In private, however, Churchill did not fully subscribe to the doctrine of "unconditional surrender," and was taken by surprise when Franklin Roosevelt announced this to the world as Allied consensus.

The settlement concerning the borders of Poland, that is, the boundary between Poland and the Soviet Union and between Germany and Poland, was viewed as a betrayal in Poland during the post-war years, as it was established against the views of the Polish government in exile. It was Winston Churchill, who tried to motivate Mikolajczyk, who was prime minister of the Polish government in exile, to accept Stalin's wishes, but Mikolajczyk refused. Churchill was convinced that the only way to alleviate tensions between the two populations was the transfer of people, to match the national borders.

As he expounded in the House of Commons on 15 December 1944, "Expulsion is the method which, insofar as we have been able to see, will be the most satisfactory and lasting. There will be no mixture of populations to cause endless trouble ... A clean sweep will be made. I am not alarmed by these transferences, which are more possible in modern conditions." However the resulting expulsions of Germans were carried out in a way which resulted in much hardship and, according to a 1966 report by the West German Ministry of Refugees and Displaced Persons, the death of over 2.1 million. Churchill opposed the effective annexation of Poland by the Soviet Union and wrote bitterly about it in his books, but he was unable to prevent it at the conferences.

During October 1944, he and Eden were in Moscow to meet with the Russian leadership. At this point, Russian forces were beginning to advance into various eastern European countries. Churchill held the view that until everything was formally and properly worked out at the Yalta conference, there had to be a temporary, war-time, working agreement with regard to who would run what. The most significant of these meetings was held on 9 October 1944 in the Kremlin between Churchill and Stalin. During the meeting, Poland and the Balkan problems were discussed.

One of the conclusions of the Yalta Conference was that

the Allies would return all Soviet citizens that found themselves in the Allied zone to the Soviet Union. This immediately affected the Soviet prisoners of war liberated by the Allies, but was also extended to all Eastern European refugees. Aleksandr Solzhenitsyn called the Operation Keelhaul "the last secret" of the Second World War. The operation decided the fate of up to two million post-war refugees fleeing eastern Europe.

Dresden bombings controversy

Between 13–15 February 1945, British and US bombers attacked the German city of Dresden, which was crowded with German wounded and refugees. There were an unknown number of refugees in Dresden, so historians Matthias Neutzner, Götz Bergander and Frederick Taylor have used historical sources and deductive reasoning to estimate that the number of refugees in the city and surrounding suburbs was around 200,000 or less on the first night of the bombing. Because of the cultural importance of the city, and of the number of civilian casualties close to the end of the war, this remains one of the most controversial Western Allied actions of the war. On reflection, under pressure from the Chiefs of Staff and in response to the views expressed by Sir Charles Portal (Chief of the Air Staff) and Sir Arthur Harris (AOC-in-C of RAF Bomber Command), among others, Churchill withdrew his memo and issued a new one. This final version of the memo completed on 1 April 1945, stated:

"It seems to me that the moment has come when the

question of the so called 'area-bombing' of German cities should be reviewed from the point of view of our own interests. If we come into control of an entirely ruined land, there will be a great shortage of accommodation for ourselves and our allies ... We must see to it that our attacks do no more harm to ourselves in the long run than they do to the enemy's war effort."

Ultimately, responsibility for the British part of the attack lay with Churchill, which is why he has been criticised for allowing the bombings to occur. German historian Jörg Friedrich claims that Churchill's decision was a "war crime", and writing in 2006 the philosopher A. C. Grayling questioned the whole strategic bombing campaign by the RAF, presenting the argument that although it was not a war crime it was a moral crime that undermines the Allies' contention that they fought a just war. On the other hand, it has also been asserted that Churchill's involvement in the bombing of Dresden was based on the strategic and tactical aspects of winning the war. The destruction of Dresden, while immense, was designed to expedite the defeat of Germany. As historian and journalist Max Hastings wrote in an article subtitled "the Allied Bombing of Dresden": "I believe it is wrong to describe strategic bombing as a war crime, for this might be held to suggest some moral equivalence with the deeds of the Nazis. Bombing represented a sincere, albeit mistaken, attempt to bring about Germany's military defeat." British historian Frederick Taylor asserts that "All sides bombed each other's cities during the war. Half a million Soviet citizens, for example, died from German bombing during the invasion and occupation of

Russia. That's roughly equivalent to the number of German citizens who died from Allied raids."

Second World War ends

In June 1944, the Allied Forces invaded Normandy and pushed the Nazi forces back into Germany on a broad front over the coming year. After being attacked on three fronts by the Allies, and in spite of Allied failures, such as Operation Market Garden, and German counter-attacks, including the Battle of the Bulge, Germany was eventually defeated. On 7 May 1945 at the SHAEF headquarters in Rheims the Allies accepted Germany's surrender. On the same day in a BBC news flash John Snagge announced that 8 May would be Victory in Europe Day. On Victory in Europe Day, Churchill broadcast to the nation that Germany had surrendered and that a final cease fire on all fronts in Europe would come into effect at one minute past midnight that night. Afterwards, Churchill told a huge crowd in Whitehall: "This is your victory." The people shouted: "No, it is yours", and Churchill then conducted them in the singing of "Land of Hope and Glory". In the evening he made another broadcast to the nation asserting the defeat of Japan in the coming months. The Japanese later surrendered on 15 August 1945.

As Europe celebrated peace at the end of six years of war, Churchill was concerned with the possibility that the celebrations would soon be brutally interrupted. He concluded that the UK and the US must anticipate the Red Army ignoring previously agreed frontiers and agreements in Europe, and prepare to "impose upon Russia the will of the United States and the British Empire." According to the Operation Unthinkable plan ordered by Churchill and developed by the British Armed Forces, the Third World War could have started on 1 July 1945 with a sudden attack against the allied Soviet troops. The plan was rejected by the British Chiefs of Staff Committee as militarily unfeasible.

Operation Unthinkable

Operation Unthinkable was a code name of two related plans of a conflict between the Western Allies and the Soviet Union. Both were ordered by British Prime Minister Winston Churchill in 1945 and developed by the British Armed Forces' Joint Planning Staff at the end of World War II in Europe.

The first of the two assumed a surprise attack on the Soviet forces stationed in Germany in order to "impose the will of the Western Allies" on the Soviets. "The will" was qualified as "square deal for Poland" (which probably meant enforcing the recently signed Yalta Agreement). When the odds were judged "fanciful", the original plan was abandoned. The code name was used instead for a defensive scenario, in which the British were to defend against a Soviet drive towards the North Sea and the Atlantic following the withdrawal of the American forces from the continent.

The study became the first Cold War-era contingency plan for war with the Soviet Union. Both plans were highly secret at the time of their creation and it was not until 1998 that they were made public.

Offensive operations

The initial primary goal of the operation was declared as follows: "to impose upon Russia the will of the United States and the British Empire. Even though 'the will' of these two countries may be defined as no more than a square deal for Poland, that does not necessarily limit the military commitment". The word "Russia" is used heavily throughout the document, as during the Imperial period the term was used to refer to the Russian Empire, with which the USSR was almost coterminous.

The Chiefs of Staff were concerned that given the enormous size of Soviet forces deployed in Europe at the end of the war, and the perception that the Soviet leader Joseph Stalin was unreliable, there existed a Soviet threat to Western Europe. The Soviet numerical superiority was roughly 4:1 in men and 2:1 in tanks at the end of hostilities in Europe. The Soviet Union had yet to launch its attack on Japanese forces, and so one assumption in the report was that the Soviet Union would instead ally with Japan if the Western Allies commenced hostilities. The hypothetical date for the start of the Allied invasion of Soviet-held Europe was scheduled for 1 July 1945. The plan assumed a surprise attack by up to 47 British and American divisions in the area of Dresden, in the middle of Soviet lines. This represented almost half of the roughly 100 divisions (approximately 2.5 million men) available to the

British, American and Canadian headquarters at that time.

The plan was taken by the British Chiefs of Staff Committee as militarily unfeasible due to a three-to-one superiority of Soviet land forces in Europe and the Middle East, where the conflict was projected to take place. The majority of any offensive operation would have been undertaken by American and British forces, as well as Polish forces and up to 100,000 German Wehrmacht soldiers. Any quick success would be due to surprise alone. If a quick success could not be obtained before the onset of winter, the assessment was that the Allies would be committed to a protracted total war. In the report of 22 May 1945, an offensive operation was deemed "hazardous".

Defensive operations

In response to an instruction by Churchill of 10 June 1945, a follow-up report was written concerning "what measures would be required to ensure the security of the British Isles in the event of war with Russia in the near future". United States forces were relocating to the Pacific for a planned invasion of Japan, and Churchill was concerned that this reduction in supporting forces would leave the Soviets in a strong position to take offensive action in Western Europe. The report concluded that if the United States focused on the Pacific Theatre, Great Britain's odds "would become fanciful."

The Joint Planning Staff rejected Churchill's notion of retaining bridgeheads on the continent as having no operational advantage. It was envisaged that Britain would use its air force and navy to resist, although a threat from mass rocket attack was anticipated, with no means of resistance except for strategic bombing.

Subsequent discussions

By 1946 tensions and conflicts were developing between Allied-occupied and Soviet-occupied areas of Europe. These were seen as being potential triggers for a wider conflict. One such area was the Julian March (which was applied to an area of southeastern Europe, today split among Croatia, Slovenia, and Italy), and on 30 August 1946 informal discussions took place between the British and US Chiefs of Staff concerning how such a conflict could develop and the best strategy for conducting a European war. Again the issue of retaining a bridgehead on the continent was discussed, with Dwight D. Eisenhower preferring a withdrawal to the Low Countries, rather than Italy, for their proximity to the United Kingdom.

LATER LIFE OF WINSTON CHURCHILL

After the end of the war Churchill had to step down as Prime Minister of the United Kingdom because the Conservative Party lost the 1945 election. For six years he was to serve as the Leader of the Opposition. During these years Churchill continued to have an impact on world affairs; in 1946 he gave his Iron Curtain speech which spoke of the expansionist policies of the USSR and the creation of the Eastern Bloc; Churchill also argued strongly for British independence from the European Coal and Steel Community (which he saw as a Franco-German project). In the General Election of 1951 Labour was defeated and Churchill became Prime Minister for a second time. Churchill continued to lead Britain but was to suffer increasingly from health problems. Aware that he was slowing down both physically and mentally he resigned from the Cabinet in 1955. However he continued to sit as an MP for Woodford until he retired from politics in 1964. Churchill died on 24 January 1965 and was granted the honour of a state funeral. He was buried in his family plot in St Martin's Church, Bladon near to where he was born at Blenheim Palace.

The 1945 Election

Although Churchill's role in World War II had generated him much support from the British population, he had many opponents. He also expressed contempt for a number of popular ideas, in particular creating a system of national public health care and improving public education. Partly as a result of this Churchill was defeated in the 1945 election by Clement Attlee and the Labour Party. There are different theories as to why he lost this election; it could be that the voters thought that the man who had led them so well in war was not the man to lead them in peace, or that the election result was not a reaction against Churchill personally, but against the Conservative Party's record in the 1930s under Baldwin and Chamberlain. Also, the proposed reformist policies of the Labour Party— such as introducing the NHS—appealed strongly to voters. During the opening broadcast of the election campaign, Churchill astonished many of his admirers by warning that a Labour government would introduce into Britain "some form of Gestapo, no doubt humanely administered in the first instance". Churchill had been genuinely worried during the war by the inroads of state bureaucracy into civil liberty, and was clearly influenced by Friedrich Hayek's anti-totalitarian tract, The Road to Serfdom (1944).

His Resignation Honours included recommendations outside of party politics for the Chiefs of Staff of the armed services and the Ministry of Defence, which had the approval of the new Prime Minister.

Leader of the opposition

Although Churchill was no longer Prime Minister, he would not leave the public eye for many years. His image as a world leader, and seasoned diplomat would allow him to remain a figurehead in British politics. Churchill became the leader of the opposition, the Conservative Party. While acting as leader Churchill accomplished a great many things, and would make his voice heard on proposals which he strongly opposed. The first major issue where Churchill made his view known was whether or not to release India from British control. In a speech to the House of Commons in early March 1947, Churchill warned against handing power over to India too soon. Churchill felt that the political parties in India did not truly represent the people, and that in a few years no trace of the new government would remain.

Winston Churchill was an early supporter of pan-Europeanism. In his speech at the University of Zurich in 1946, Winston Churchill called for a "United States of Europe" and the creation of a "Council of Europe". He also participated in the Hague Congress of 1948, which discussed the future structure and role of this Council of Europe. The Council of Europe was finally founded as the first European institution through the Treaty of London of 5 May 1949 and has its seat in Strasbourg.

According to a memorandum from the FBI's archives, in 1947 Winston Churchill urged the US to conduct a preemptive nuclear strike against the Soviet Union in order to win the

Cold War, before it's too late. Churchill reportedly spoke to right-wing Republican senator Styles Bridges, asking him to persuade then-President Harry Truman to launch a nuclear strike against Kremlin, wiping it out, which would then make it easy to handle the directionless Russia. The memorandum claims Churchill "stated that the only salvation for the civilization of the world would be if the President of the United States would declare Russia to be imperiling world peace and attack Russia". Russia would have been defenseless against a nuclear strike at the time of the Churchill's proposal, since the Soviets did not obtain the atomic bomb until 1949.

The Second premiership

After the General Election of 1951, Churchill again became Prime Minister. His third government—after the wartime national government and the brief caretaker government of 1945—would last until his resignation in 1955. During this period, he renewed what he called the "special relationship" between Britain and the United States, and engaged himself in the formation of the post-war order. He tried in vain to manoeuvre the cabinet into restricting West Indian immigration. "Keep England White" was a good slogan, he told the cabinet in January 1955. Ian Gilmour records Churchill saying to him, in 1955, about immigration: "I think it is the most important subject facing this country, but I cannot get any of my ministers to take any notice". In what would become one of Churchill's most famous speeches, the Fulton Speech would coin a phrase which would be used for the remainder of the Cold War. The iron curtain is what Churchill referred to the Soviet Union's growing influence in Eastern Europe. At the time that Churchill made the speech both the United States and his own government publicly disagreed with him. His speech would later be hailed as having great prophetic value. Later it would be shown that President Truman and the Prime Minister both shared Churchill's feelings, but felt they could not disclose this publicly.

Churchill would coin another famous term, this time relating to the relationship between the United States and Britain. This term "special relationship" referred to the closeness of the Anglo-American connection in war, peace, and in politics. The relationship had fluctuated during the histories of the two countries, but had been visibly stronger in the 20th century, especially during World War II. Churchill played a major role in the "special relationship", becoming what appeared to be close friends with Roosevelt during the war years. Churchill would later try to regain this relationship with President Truman.

His domestic priorities were, however, overshadowed by a series of foreign policy crises, which were partly the result of the continued decline of British military and imperial prestige and power. Being a strong proponent of Britain as an international power, Churchill would often propose to meet such crises with direct action. In 1941, during World War II, he had stated, "I did not become Prime Minister to preside over a dismemberment of the British Empire." Churchill devoted much of his time in office to international relations and although Churchill did not get on well with President Dwight D. Eisenhower, Churchill in attempting to maintain the special relationship made four official transatlantic visits to America during his second term as Prime-Minister.

When President Eisenhower was elected in 1952, Churchill made haste in arranging a meeting with the new leader in hopes of establishing a stronger relationship with the United States. This would prove to be nearly impossible, due to Churchill's age. He was beginning to show losses of faculty, and allegedly refused to wear his hearing aid while in meetings, causing the conversations to be carried on at a screaming volume. Eisenhower remarked in his diary how Churchill seemed set in his ways, and that Churchill seemed to think that the world's problems could be solved merely by the close cooperation of Britain and the United States.

Churchill would also try to establish better relations with the Soviet Union when, in 1953, Stalin died. He saw the death of Stalin to mean that the Soviet Union would be under far better leadership than it had been, and that the opportunity to establish better British-Soviet relations should be seized. Unfortunately for Churchill, the United States as well as his own party saw this unilateral action as hasty.

The Mau Mau Rebellion

In 1951, grievances against the colonial distribution of land came to a head with the Kenya African Union demanding greater representation and land reform. When these demands were rejected, more radical elements came forward, launching the Mau Mau rebellion in 1952. On 20 October 1952, a state of emergency was declared, and British troops were flown to Kenya to deal with the rebellion. As both sides increased the ferocity of their attacks, the country moved to full-scale civil war.

In 1953, the Lari massacre, perpetrated by Mau-Mau insurgents against Kikuyu loyal to the British, changed the political complexion of the rebellion and gave the public-relations advantage to the British. Churchill's strategy was to use a military response, combined with implementing many of the concessions that Attlee's government had blocked in 1951. He ordered an increased military presence and appointed General Sir George Erskine, who would implement Operation Anvil in 1954 that defeated the rebellion in the city of Nairobi. Churchill ordered peace talks to be opened, but these collapsed shortly after his leaving office.

Malayan Emergency

In Malaya, a rebellion against British rule had been in progress since 1948. Once again, Churchill's government inherited a crisis, and once again Churchill chose to use direct military action against those in rebellion while attempting to build an alliance with those who were not. He stepped up the implementation of a "hearts and minds" campaign and approved the creation of fortified villages, a tactic that would become a recurring part of Western military strategy in South-east Asia.

The Malayan Emergency was a more direct case of a guerrilla movement, centred in an ethnic group, but backed by the Soviet Union. As such, Britain's policy of direct confrontation and military victory had a great deal more support than in Iran or in Kenya. At the high point of the conflict, over 40,000 British and Commonwealth troops were stationed in Malaya. While the rebellion was slowly being defeated, it was equally clear that colonial rule from Britain was no longer plausible. In 1953, plans were drawn up for independence for Malaya, Singapore and the other crown colonies in the region. The first elections were held in 1955, just days before Churchill's own resignation, and in 1957, under Prime Minister Harold Macmillan, Malaya became independent.

The Secret disability crisis of 1953

Churchill had suffered a mild stroke while on holiday in the south of France in the summer of 1949. The strain of carrying the Premiership and Foreign Office contributed to his stroke at 10 Downing Street after dinner on the evening of 23 June 1953. Despite being partially paralysed down one side, he presided over a Cabinet meeting the next morning without anybody noticing his incapacity. Thereafter his condition deteriorated, and it was thought that he might not survive the weekend. Had Eden been fit, Churchill's premiership would most likely have been over. News of this was kept from the public and from Parliament, who were told that Churchill was suffering from exhaustion. He went to his country home, Chartwell, to recuperate, and by the end of June he astonished his doctors by being able, dripping with perspiration, to lift himself upright from his chair. He joked that news of his illness had chased the trial of the serial killer John Christie off the front pages.

Foreign relations and the Cold War

Churchill was still keen to pursue a meeting with the Soviets and was open to the idea of a reunified Germany. He refused to condemn the Soviet crushing of East Germany, commenting on 10 July 1953 that "The Russians were surprisingly patient about the disturbances in East Germany". He thought this might have been the reason for the removal of Beria. Churchill returned to public life in October 1953 to make a speech at the Conservative Party conference at Margate. In December 1953 Churchill met Eisenhower in Bermuda.

Churchill was cross about friction between Eden and Dulles (June 1954). On the trip home from another Anglo-American conference, the diplomat Pierson Dixon compared US actions in Guatemala to Soviet policy in Korea and Greece, causing Churchill to retort that Guatemala was a "bloody place" he'd "never heard of". Churchill was still keen for a trip to Moscow, and threatened to resign, provoking a crisis in the Cabinet when Lord Salisbury threatened to resign if Churchill had his way. In the end the Soviets proposed a five power conference, which did not meet until after Churchill had retired. By the autumn Churchill was again postponing his resignation. Eden, now partly recovered from his operations, became a major figure on the world stage in 1954, helping to negotiate peace in Indo-China, an agreement with Egypt and to broker an agreement between the countries of Western Europe after the French rejection of the EDC.

Resignation

Aware that he was slowing down both physically and mentally, Churchill at last retired as prime minister in 1955 and was succeeded by Anthony Eden. He suffered another mild stroke in December 1956.

Later life

Churchill's fondness for alcohol was well documented. While in India and South Africa, he got in the habit of adding small amounts of whisky to the water he drank in order to prevent disease. He was quoted on the subject as saying that "by dint of careful application I learned to like it." He consumed alcoholic drinks on a near-daily basis for long periods in his life, and frequently imbibed before, after, and during mealtimes, although he is not generally considered by historians to have been an alcoholic. The Churchill Centre states that Churchill made a bet with a man with the last name of Rothermere (possibly one of the Viscounts Rothermere) in 1936 that Churchill would be able to successfully abstain from drinking hard liquor for a year; Churchill apparently won the bet.

Aware that he was slowing down both physically and mentally, Churchill retired as Prime Minister in 1955 and was succeeded by Anthony Eden, who had long been his ambitious protégé (three years earlier, Eden had married Churchill's niece, Anne Clarissa Spencer-Churchill, his second marriage). Shortly preceding his resignation, Churchill experienced an extended bout of somnambulism, a condition to which he was prone. Upon his resignation, the Queen offered him a dukedom but he declined the offer.

Over the coming years, Churchill spent less time in Parliament, occasionally voting in parliamentary divisions but never again speaking in the House. He continued to serve as MP for Woodford until he stood down for the last time at the 1964 General Election. His private verdict on the Suez fiasco was: "I would never have done it without squaring the Americans, and once I'd started I'd never have dared stop". In 1959, he became Father of the House, the MP with the longest continuous service: he had already gained the distinction of being the only MP to be elected under both Queen Victoria and Queen Elizabeth II. On 27 July 1964, Churchill was present in the House of Commons for the last time, and one day later, on 28 July, a deputation headed by the Prime Minister, Sir Alec Douglas-Home, presented Churchill with a Resolution which had been carried nemine contradicente by the House of Commons. The ceremony was held in Churchill's London home at 28 Hyde Park Gate, and was witnessed by Clementine and his children and grandchildren.

Churchill spent most of his retirement at Chartwell House in Kent, two miles (3 km) south of Westerham. As Churchill's mental and physical faculties decayed, it is often suggested, he began to lose the battle he had fought for so long against the "black dog" of (clinical) depression. However, the biographical evidence, when carefully and comprehensively studied, suggests that "black dog" is more accurately interpreted as Churchill's metaphor for the temporary, non-disabling psychological reactions of worry and anxiety that he manifested throughout his career following severely adverse difficulties and setbacks. The unfailing remedy for him at such times, which he discovered in 1915, was painting; later on, he added bricklaying at Chartwell to his armamentarium. In advanced old age, his faculties too impaired to enable him to paint, he found some solace in the sunshine and colours of the Mediterranean. He took long holidays with his literary adviser Emery Reves and Emery's wife, Wendy Russell, at La Pausa, their villa on the French Riviera, seldom joined by Clementine. He also took eight cruises aboard the yacht Christina as the guest of Aristotle Onassis. Once, when the Christina had to pass through the Dardanelles, Onassis gave instructions that it was to do so during the night, so as not to disturb his guest with unhappy memories.

In 1963, US President John F. Kennedy, acting under authorisation granted by an Act of Congress, proclaimed Churchill the first Honorary Citizen of the United States. Churchill was physically incapable of attending the White House ceremony, so his son and grandson accepted the award for him. As his family life grew more despondent (he was unable to resolve the love-hate relationship between himself and his son) Churchill was also to suffer a further two strokes during the 1960s. On 15 January 1965, Churchill suffered another stroke, this time a severe cerebral thrombosis that left him gravely ill. He died at his home nine days later, at age 90, shortly after eight o'clock on the morning of Sunday 24 January 1965, coincidentally 70 years to the day after his father's death. After his death, Churchill's body was embalmed at his London home by Desmond Henley.

Funeral

By decree of the Queen, his body lay in state in Westminster Hall for three days and a state funeral service was held at St Paul's Cathedral. This was the first state funeral for a non-royal-family member since 1914.

The procession moved to Tower Pier where the coffin was taken on board the MV Havengore. Naval ratings 'piped the side' and the Royal Marine band played the musical salute due to a former First Lord of the Admiralty, Rule Britannia. As his coffin passed up the Thames, dockers lowered their crane jibs in a salute. The Royal Artillery fired a 19-gun salute (as head of government and as Lord Warden of the Cinque Ports), and the RAF staged a fly-past of sixteen English Electric Lightning fighters.

The state funeral was the largest gathering of dignitaries in Britain, as representatives from well over 100 countries attended, including French President Charles de Gaulle, Canadian Prime Minister Lester B. Pearson, Prime Minister of Rhodesia Ian Smith, former US president Dwight Eisenhower, and many other heads of state, including past and present heads of state and government, and members of royal families the world over. The Prime Minister of Australia, Sir Robert Menzies, then the longest serving Commonwealth Prime Minister (who had known Churchill intimately in wartime), paid tribute to his colleague as part of the funeral broadcast, as did President Eisenhower. The train was hauled by the Battle of Britain class locomotive 34051 Winston Churchill. Fittingly, this was the last great State occasion to be movingly commented upon by the great British broadcaster Richard Dimbleby, who died of lung cancer in December 1965. The funeral also saw the largest assemblage of statesmen in the world since the funeral of President John F. Kennedy in 1963.

At Churchill's request, he was buried in the family plot at St Martin's Church, Bladon, near Woodstock, not far from his birthplace at Blenheim. In the fields along the route, and at the stations through which the train passed, thousands stood in silence to pay their last respects. In 1998 his tombstone had to be replaced due to the large number of visitors over the years having eroded it and its surrounding area. A new stone was dedicated in 1998 in a ceremony attended by members of the Spencer-Churchill family.

Because the funeral took place on 30 January, people in the United States marked it by paying tribute to his friendship with Franklin D. Roosevelt because it was the anniversary of FDR's birth. Those who attended a service at Roosevelt's grave at his home in Hyde Park, New York, heard speakers at the service talk about the coincidence of the date in the records of two leaders who shared history.

On 9 February 1965, Churchill's estate was probated at £304,044 (£5.26 million as of 2016). Churchill left £10,000 to Anthony Montague Browne, his private secretary, and returned a gold cigarette case given to him by Earl of Birkenhead to the current "holder of that title". Three "brood mares, followers or fillies not exceeding £7500 in value" were given to Christopher Soames, Baron Soames, his son-in-law.

CHURCHILL AS A WRITER & HISTORIAN

Winston Churchill was a prolific writer, under the pen name "Winston S. Churchill". Churchill received the Nobel Prize in Literature in 1953 for his numerous published works, especially his six-volume work The Second World War. At the ceremony he was awarded the prize "for his mastery of historical and biographical description as well as for brilliant oratory in defending exalted human values."

Churchill's first paid work as a writer was for a series of five articles on the Cuban War of Independence in The Graphic in 1895, the year of his father Lord Randolph's death. For the rest of his life, writing was Churchill's main income source. Almost always well paid as an author, he wrote an estimated eight to ten million words in more than 40 books, thousands of newspaper and magazine articles, and at least two film scripts. His first published book was The Story of the Malakand Field Force. It details an 1897 military campaign on the Northwest Frontier (an area now part of Pakistan and Afghanistan).

Churchill's second book, The River War, was an account

of the British reconquest of the Sudan, written in 1899 while he was still an officer in the British army. The book provides a history of the British involvement in the Sudan and the conflict between the British forces led by Lord Kitchener and Islamic Jihadists led by a self-proclaimed second prophet of Islam Muhammad Ahmad who had embarked on a campaign to conquer Egypt, to drive out the non-Muslim infidels and make way for the second coming of the Islamic Mahdi. Churchill was himself present at the Battle of Omdurman which is described as part of the history.

The Second World War is a six-volume history of the period from the end of the First World War to July 1945. The most ambitious of any work published by Churchill, it was to take a great portion of his life following his defeat in the 1945 post war election. The first volume was published in 1948 but the work was not finished until 1953. The work was one of Churchill's writings mentioned in his Nobel Prize in literature citation. A History of the English-Speaking Peoples is a four-volume history of Britain and its former colonies and possessions throughout the world, covering the period from Caesar's invasions of Britain (55 BC) to the beginning of the First World War (1914). It was started in 1937 and finally published 1956–58, delayed several times by war and his work on other texts.

Churchill's view of history

Churchill was an exponent of the view that the British and American people had a unique greatness and destiny and that all British history should be seen as progress towards fulfilling that destiny. This belief inspired his political career as well as his historical writing.

Although Churchill was not a trained historian, the influences on his historical thought and prose style, were likely Clarendon's history of the English Civil War, Gibbon's Decline and Fall and Macaulay's History of England.

The second category is Churchill's autobiographical works, including his early journalistic compilations The Story of the Malakand Field Force (1898), The River War (1899), London to Ladysmith via Pretoria (1900) and Ian Hamilton's March (1900). These latter two were issued in a re-edited form as My Early Life (1930). All of these books contain information about Britain's imperial wars in India, Sudan and South Africa. The works on South Africa contain elements of self-promotion, since Churchill was a candidate for Parliament in 1900.

These four books were republished as Frontiers and Wars: His Four Early Books Covering His Life As Soldier and War Correspondent, New York: Harcourt, Brace & World, Inc., 1962.

Churchill's reputation as a writer, however, rests on his multi-volume works of narrative history: The World Crisis (six volumes, 1923–31), and of The Second World War (six volumes, 1948–53), and his A History of the English-Speaking Peoples (four volumes, 1956–58, much of which had been written as journalism in the 1930s). These are among the longest works of history ever published (The Second World War runs to more than two million words), and earned him the Nobel Prize in Literature.

Churchill's histories of the two world wars were based on the author's status as a central participant in both stories. Although both are memoirs as well as histories, Churchill was careful to broaden their scope to include events in which he played no part—the war between Nazi Germany and the Soviet Union, for example. Inevitably, however, Churchill placed Britain, and therefore himself, at the centre of his narrative. Arthur Balfour described The World Crisis as "Winston's brilliant autobiography, disguised as a history of the universe." In any case he had far fewer documentary sources for matters not involving Britain.

As a Cabinet minister for part of the First World War and as Prime Minister for nearly all of the Second, Churchill had unique access to official documents, military plans, official secrets and correspondence between world leaders. After the First War, when there were few rules governing these documents, Churchill simply took many of them with him when he left office, and used them freely in his books, particularly for The World Crisis. This was done by other wartime ministers such as David Lloyd George, but, following the First World War, stricter rules were put in place regarding Cabinet documents.

The World Crisis began as a response to Lord Esher's attack

on his reputation in his memoirs, but it soon broadened out into a general multi-volume history. The volumes are a mix of military history, written with Churchill's usual narrative flair, diplomatic and political history, portraits of other political and military figures, and personal memoir, written in a colourful manner.

When he resumed office in 1939, Churchill fully intended to write a history of the war then beginning. He said several times: "I will leave judgements on this matter to history—but I will be one of the historians." To circumvent the rules against the use of official documents, he took the precaution throughout the war of having a weekly summary of correspondence, minutes, memoranda and other documents printed in galleys and headed "Prime Minister's personal minutes". As well, Churchill actually wrote or dictated a number of letters and memoranda with the specific intention of placing his views on the record for later use as a historian.

REFERENCES

- *Churchill, Winston. The World Crisis. Six vols. (1923–31); one-vol. ed. (2005). On the First World War.*

- *Churchill, Winston. The Second World War. Six vols. (1948–53)*

- *Coombs, David, ed., with Minnie Churchill. Sir Winston Churchill: His Life through His Paintings. Fwd. by Mary Soames. Pegasus, 2003. ISBN 0-7624-2731-0. Other editions entitled Sir Winston Churchill's Life and His Paintings and Sir Winston Churchill: His Life and His Paintings. Includes illustrations of approx. 500–534 paintings by Churchill.*

- *Edwards, Ron. Eastcote: From Village to Suburb (1987). Uxbridge: London Borough of Hillingdon. ISBN 0-907869-09-2.*

- *Gilbert, Martin. In Search of Churchill: A Historian's Journey (1994). Memoir about editing the following multi-volume work.*

- *Gilbert, Martin, ed. Winston S. Churchill. An eight-volume biography begun by Randolph Churchill, supported by 15 companion vols. of official and unofficial documents relating to Churchill. 1966–*

  - *I. Youth, 1874–1900 (2 vols., 1966);*

  - *II. Young Statesman, 1901–1914 (3 vols., 1967);*

- *III. The Challenge of War, 1914–1916 (3 vols., 1973). ISBN 0-395-16974-7 (10) and ISBN 978-0-395-16974-2 (13);*

- *IV. The Stricken World, 1916–1922 (2 vols., 1975);*

- *V. The Prophet of Truth, 1923–1939 (3 vols., 1977);*

- *VI. Finest Hour, 1939–1941: The Churchill War Papers (2 vols., 1983);*

- *VII. Road to Victory, 1941–1945 (4 vols., 1986);*

- *VIII. Never Despair, 1945–1965 (3 vols., 1988).*

- *James, Robert Rhodes, ed. Winston S. Churchill: His Complete Speeches, 1897–1963. Eight vols. London: Chelsea, 1974.*

- *Knowles, Elizabeth. The Oxford Dictionary of Twentieth Century Quotations. Oxford, Eng.: Oxford University Press, 1999. ISBN 0-19-860103-4. ISBN 978-0-19-860103-6. ISBN 0-19-866250-5. ISBN 978-0-19-866250-1.*

- *Langworth, Richard, ed. Churchill in his own Words, Ebury Press, 2008. ISBN 978-0-09-193336-4*

- *Loewenheim, Francis L. and Harold D. Langley, eds (1975). Roosevelt and Churchill: Their Secret Wartime Correspondence.*

- *Beschloss, Michael R. (2002). The Conquerors: Roosevelt, Truman and the Destruction of Hitler's Germany, 1941–1945. New York: Simon & Schuster. ISBN 978-0-684-81027-0. OCLC 50315054.*

- *Best, Geoffrey (2003) [First published 2001]. Churchill: A Study in Greatness. Oxford: Oxford University Press. ISBN 978-1-85285-253-5. OCLC 50339762.*

- *Blake, Robert (1997). Winston Churchill. Pocket Biographies. Stroud: Sutton Publishing. ISBN 978-0-7509-1507-6. OCLC 59586004.*

- *Blake, Robert; Louis, William Roger, eds. (1992). Churchill: A Major New Reassessment of His Life in Peace and War. Oxford: Oxford University Press. ISBN 978-0-19-282317-5. OCLC 30029512.*

- *Browne, Anthony Montague (1995). Long sunset : memoirs of Winston Churchill's last private secretary. London: Cassell. ISBN 978-0-304-34478-9. OCLC 32547047.*

- *Charmley, John (1993). Churchill, The End of Glory: A Political Biography. London: Hodder & Stoughton. ISBN 978-0-15-117881-0. OCLC 440131865.*

- *harmley, John (1996). Churchill's Grand Alliance: The Anglo-American Special Relationship 1940–57. London: Hodder & Stoughton. ISBN 978-0-340-59760-6. OCLC 247165348.*

- *Davis, Richard Harding. Real Soldiers of Fortune (1906). Early biography. Project Gutenberg etext, wikisource here "Real Soldiers of Fortune/Chapter 3". En.wikisource.org. 20 October 2007. Retrieved 9 August 2009.*

- *D'Este, Carlo (2008). Warlord: a life of Winston Churchill at war, 1874–1945 (1st ed.). New York: Harper. ISBN 978-0-06-057573-1. Retrieved 26 November 2008.*

- *Fisher, Nigel (1982). Harold Macmillan. London: Weidenfeld and Nicolson. ISBN 978-0-297-77914-8.*

- *Gilbert, Martin. Churchill: A Life (1992); ISBN 0-8050-*

2396-8 One-volume version of 8-volume biography

- Haffner, Sebastian. *Winston Churchill (1967)*

- Hastings, Max. *Finest Years: Churchill as Warlord, 1940–45.* London: HarperPress, 2009; ISBN 978-0-00-726367-7

- Hennessy, P. *Prime minister: the office and its holders since 1945 (2001).*

- Hitchens, Christopher. "The Medals of His Defeats", *The Atlantic Monthly (April 2002)*

- Irving, David. "Churchill's War – Vol. 1: The Struggle for Power", London: Veritas Books, 1987; ISBN 978-0947117566; "Churchill's War – Vol. 2:Triumph in Adversity"; London: Focal Point Publications; First edition (September 1, 2001); ISBN 978-1872197159.

- James, Robert Rhodes. *Churchill: A Study in Failure, 1900–1939 (1970)* ISBN 978-0-29-782015-4

- Jenkins, Roy. *Churchill: A Biography (2001); ISBN 978-0-374-12354-3/ISBN 978-0-452-28352-7*

- Johnson, Boris, *The Churchill Factor: How One Man Made History.* Hodder & Stoughton, 2013. ISBN 978-1444783025

- Jordan, Anthony J. *Churchill: A Founder of Modern Ireland.* Westport Books (1995); ISBN 978-0-9524447-0-1

- Julius, Anthony, *The Trials of the Diaspora, A History of Anti-Semitism in England.* Oxford University Press, 2010. ISBN 978-0-19-929705-4

- Kersaudy, François. *Churchill and De Gaulle (1981); ISBN*

0-00-216328-4

- *Krockow, Christian. Churchill: Man of the Century. [1900–1999]; ISBN 1-902809-43-2*

- *Lukacs, John. Churchill: Visionary, Statesman, Historian. New Haven: Yale University Press, 2002*

- *Manchester, William. The Last Lion: Winston Spencer Churchill: Alone, 1932–1940 (1988); ISBN 0-316-54512-0*

- *Manchester, William. The Last Lion: Winston Spencer Churchill: Defender of the Realm, 1940–1965 (2010)*

- *Manchester, William. The Last Lion: Winston Spencer Churchill: Visions of Glory, 1874–1932 (1983); ISBN 0-316-54503-1*

- *Massie, Robert. Dreadnought: Britain, Germany, and the Coming of the Great War; ISBN 1-84413-528-4 [chapters 40–41 concern Churchill at Admiralty.]*

- *Pelling, Henry. Winston Churchill (1974); ISBN 1-84022-218-2. [Comprehensive biography]*

- *Rasor, Eugene L. Winston S. Churchill, 1874–1965: A Comprehensive Historiography and Annotated Bibliography. Greenwood Press, 2000; ISBN 0-313-30546-3 [Entries include several thousand books and scholarly articles]*

- *Seldon, Anthony (1981). Churchill's Indian Summer. London: Hodder & Stoughton. ISBN 978-0340254561. [Study of the 1951–55 Government]*

- *Soames, Mary (ed.) Speaking for Themselves: The Personal*

Letters of Winston and Clementine Churchill (1998)

- *Stansky, Peter, ed. Churchill: A Profile (1973) [Perspectives on Churchill by leading scholars]*

- *Toye, Richard. Churchill's Empire: The World that Made Him and the World He Made. Macmillan. 2010; ISBN 978-0-230-70384-1*

- *Trukhanovskii, Vladimir Grigor'evich. Winston Churchill. Moscow: Progress Publishers (1978; revised edition)*

- *Olivier Weber, War Correspondent, Preface of The Malakand War, Belles Lettres (2012)*

- *Michael R. Beschloss, (2002) The Conquerors: Roosevelt, Truman and the Destruction of Hitler's Germany, 1941–1945 p. 131.*

- *Geoffrey Best. Churchill: A Study in Greatness (2003)*

- *Blake, Robert. Winston Churchill. Pocket Biographies (1997), 110 pages*

- *Blake, Robert and Louis William Roger, eds. Churchill: A Major New Reassessment of His Life in Peace and War Oxford UP, 1992, 581 pp; 29 essays by scholars*

- *John Charmley, Churchill, The End of Glory: A Political Biography (1993). revisionist; favours Chamberlain; says Churchill weakened Britain*

- *John Charmley. Churchill's Grand Alliance: The Anglo-American Special Relationship 1940–57 (1996)*

- *Richard Harding Davis, Real Soldiers of Fortune 1906, early biography. Project Gutenberg etext*

- *Martin Gilbert Churchill: A Life (1992) (ISBN 0-8050-2396-8); one volume version of 8-volume life (8900 pp); amazing detail but as Rasor complains, "no background, no context, no comment, no analysis, no judgments, no evaluation, and no insights."*

- *Sebastian Haffner, Winston Churchill 1967*

- *P. Hennessy, Prime minister: the office and its holders since 1945 2001*

- *Christopher Hitchens, "The Medals of His Defeats," The Atlantic April 2002.*

- *James, Robert Rhodes. Churchill: A Study in Failure, 1900–1939 (1970), 400 pp.*

- *Roy Jenkins. Churchill: A Biography (2001)*

- *François Kersaudy, Churchill and De Gaulle 1981 ISBN 0-00-216328-4.*

- *Christian Krockow, Churchill: Man of the Century by 2000 ISBN 1-902809-43-2.*

- *John Lukacs. Churchill: Visionary, Statesman, Historian Yale University Press, 2002.*

- *William Manchester, The Last Lion: Winston Spencer Churchill, Visions of Glory 1874–1932, 1983; ISBN 0-316-54503-1; The Last Lion: Winston Spencer Churchill, Alone 1932–1940, 1988 ISBN 0-316-54512-0; no more published*

- *Robert Massie, Dreadnought: Britain, Germany, and the Coming of the Great War (ISBN 1-84413-528-4); ch 40–41 on*

Churchill at Admiralty

- *A. Montague Browne, Long sunset 1995*

- *Kagan, Robert, (2006) Dangerous Nation (New York: Alfred A. Knopf), pp. 357–416*

- *Krohn, Jonathan. (May 2008) Review: "Caught in the Middle" -John Lawrence Tone. War and Genocide in Cuba 1895-1898 (2006), H-Net, May 2008*

- *McCartney, Paul T. (2006) Power and Progress: American National Identity, the War of 1898, and the Rise of American Imperialism (Baton Rouge: Louisiana State University Press), 87-142*

- *Silbey, David J. (2007) A War of Frontier and Empire: The Philippine-American War, 1899-1902 (New York: Hill and Wang), pp. 31–34.*

- *Tone, John Lawrence. (2006) War and Genocide in Cuba 1895-1898, Chapel Hill: University of North Carolina excerpt and text search*

- *Trask, David F. The War with Spain in 1898 (1996) ch 1 excerpt and text search*

- *Henry Pelling, Winston Churchill (first issue) 1974, (ISBN 1-84022-218-2), 736 pp; comprehensive biography*

- *Rasor, Eugene L. Winston S. Churchill, 1874-1965: A Comprehensive Historiography and Annotated Bibliography. Greenwood Press, 2000. 710 pp. describes several thousand books and scholarly articles.*

- *Stansky, Peter, ed. Churchill: A Profile 1973, 270 pp. essays for and against Churchill by leading scholars*

- *Maier, Thomas (2014), When Lions Roar: The Churchills and the Kennedys, Crown, ISBN 0307956792*

- *Churchill, Sir Winston. His life through his paintings, David Coombs, Pegasus, (2003)*

- *Churchill, Winston. The World Crisis (six volumes, 1923–31), 1-vol edition (2005); on World War I*

- *Churchill, Winston. The Second World War (six volumes, 1948–53)*

- *Gilbert, Martin, ed. Winston S. Churchill: Companion 15 vol (14,000 pages) of Churchill and other official and unofficial documents. Part 1: I. Youth, 1874–1900, 1966, 654 pp. (2 vol); II. Young Statesman, 1901–1914, 1967, 796 pp. (3 vol); III. The Challenge of War, 1914–1916, 1971, 1024 pp. (3 vol); IV. The Stricken World, 1916–1922, 1975, 984 pp. (2 vol); Part 2: The Prophet of Truth, 1923–1939, 1977, 1195 pp. (3 vol); II. Finest Hour, 1939–1941, 1983, 1328 pp. (2 vol entitled The Churchill War Papers); III. Road to Victory, 1941–1945, 1986, 1437 pp. (not published, 4 volumes are anticipated); IV. Never Despair, 1945–1965, 1988, 1438 pp. (not published, 3 volumes anticipated). See the editor's memoir, Martin Gilbert, In Search of Churchill: A Historian's Journey, (1994).*

- *James, Robert Rhodes, ed. Winston S. Churchill: His Complete Speeches, 1897–1963. 8 vols. London: Chelsea, 1974, 8917 pp.*

- *Soames, Mary, ed. Speaking for Themselves: The Personal Letters of Winston and Clementine Churchill 1998, 702 pp.*

- *Quotations database, World Beyond Borders.*

- *The Oxford Dictionary of 20th century Quotations by Oxford University Press (ISBN 0-19-860103-4)*

- *Michael R. Beschloss, (2002) The Conquerors: Roosevelt, Truman and the Destruction of Hitler's Germany, 1941–1945 p. 131.*

- *Geoffrey Best. Churchill: A Study in Greatness (2003)*

- *Blake, Robert. Winston Churchill. Pocket Biographies (1997), 110 pages*

- *Blake, Robert and Louis William Roger, eds. Churchill: A Major New Reassessment of His Life in Peace and War Oxford UP, 1992, 581 pp; 29 essays by scholars*

- *John Charmley, Churchill, The End of Glory: A Political Biography (1993). revisionist; favours Chamberlain; says Churchill weakened Britain*

- *John Charmley. Churchill's Grand Alliance: The Anglo-American Special Relationship 1940–57 (1996)*

- *Richard Harding Davis, Real Soldiers of Fortune 1906, early biography. Project Gutenberg etext*

- *Martin Gilbert Churchill: A Life (1992) (ISBN 0-8050-2396-8); one volume version of 8-volume life (8900 pp); amazing detail but as Rasor complains, "no background, no context, no comment, no analysis, no judgments, no evaluation, and no insights."*

- *Sebastian Haffner, Winston Churchill 1967*

- *P. Hennessy, Prime minister: the office and its holders since*

1945 2001

* *Christopher Hitchens, "The Medals of His Defeats," The Atlantic April 2002.*

* *James, Robert Rhodes. Churchill: A Study in Failure, 1900–1939 (1970), 400 pp.*

* *Churchill, Sir Winston. His life through his paintings, David Coombs, Pegasus, (2003)*

* *Churchill, Winston. The World Crisis (six volumes, 1923–31), 1-vol edition (2005); on World War I*

* *Churchill, Winston. The Second World War (six volumes, 1948–53)*

* *Gilbert, Martin, ed. Winston S. Churchill: Companion 15 vol (14,000 pages) of Churchill and other official and unofficial documents. Part 1: I. Youth, 1874–1900, 1966, 654 pp. (2 vol); II. Young Statesman, 1901–1914, 1967, 796 pp. (3 vol); III. The Challenge of War, 1914–1916, 1971, 1024 pp. (3 vol); IV. The Stricken World, 1916–1922, 1975, 984 pp. (2 vol); Part 2: The Prophet of Truth, 1923–1939, 1977, 1195 pp. (3 vol); II. Finest Hour, 1939–1941, 1983, 1328 pp. (2 vol entitled The Churchill War Papers); III. Road to Victory, 1941–1945, 1986, 1437 pp. (not published, 4 volumes are anticipated); IV. Never Despair, 1945–1965, 1988, 1438 pp. (not published, 3 volumes anticipated). See the editor's memoir, Martin Gilbert, In Search of Churchill: A Historian's Journey, (1994).*

* *James, Robert Rhodes, ed. Winston S. Churchill: His Complete Speeches, 1897–1963. 8 vols. London: Chelsea, 1974, 8917 pp.*

- Soames, Mary, ed. *Speaking for Themselves: The Personal Letters of Winston and Clementine Churchill 1998, 702 pp.*

- *Quotations database, World Beyond Borders.*

- *The Oxford Dictionary of 20th century Quotations by Oxford University Press (ISBN 0-19-860103-4)*

- *Roy Jenkins. Churchill: A Biography (2001)*

- *François Kersaudy, Churchill and De Gaulle 1981 ISBN 0-00-216328-4.*

- *Christian Krockow, Churchill: Man of the Century by 2000 ISBN 1-902809-43-2.*

- *John Lukacs. Churchill: Visionary, Statesman, Historian Yale University Press, 2002.*

- *William Manchester, The Last Lion: Winston Spencer Churchill, Visions of Glory 1874–1932, 1983; ISBN 0-316-54503-1; The Last Lion: Winston Spencer Churchill, Alone 1932–1940, 1988 ISBN 0-316-54512-0; no more published*

- *Robert Massie, Dreadnought: Britain, Germany, and the Coming of the Great War (ISBN 1-84413-528-4); ch 40–41 on Churchill at Admiralty*

- *A. Montague Browne, Long sunset 1995*

- *Henry Pelling, Winston Churchill (first issue) 1974, (ISBN 1-84022-218-2), 736 pp; comprehensive biography*

- *Rasor, Eugene L. Winston S. Churchill, 1874-1965: A Comprehensive Historiography and Annotated Bibliography. Greenwood Press, 2000. 710 pp. describes several thousand books and scholarly articles.*

- *Stansky, Peter, ed. Churchill: A Profile 1973, 270 pp. essays for and against Churchill by leading scholars*

- *Maier, Thomas (2014), When Lions Roar: The Churchills and the Kennedys, Crown, ISBN 0307956792*

Zofia Stone, is a freelance journalist and loves writing about famous historical figures.

CPSIA information can be obtained
at www.ICGtesting.com
Printed in the USA
LVHW091321180121
676796LV00006B/168

9 789386 019509